To

From

Date

The quoted ideas expressed in this book (but not Scripture verses) are not, in all cases, exact quotations, as some have been edited for clarity and brevity. In all cases, the author has attempted to maintain the speaker's original intent. In some cases, quoted material for this book was obtained from secondary sources, primarily print media. While every effort was made to ensure the accuracy of these sources, the accuracy cannot be guaranteed. For additions, deletions, corrections, or clarifications in future editions of this text, please write Freeman-Smith.

Scripture quotations are taken from:

The Holy Bible, King James Version (KJV)

The Holy Bible, New International Version (NIV) Copyright © 1973, 1978, 1984, by International Bible Society. Used by permission of Zondervan Publishing House. All rights reserved.

The Holy Bible, New King James Version (NKJV) Copyright © 1982 by Thomas Nelson, Inc. Used by permission.

Holy Bible, New Living Translation, (NLT) copyright © 1996. Used by permission of Tyndale House Publishers, Inc., Wheaton, Illinois 60189. All rights reserved.

The Message (MSG)- This edition issued by contractual arrangement with NavPress, a division of The Navigators, U.S.A. Originally published by NavPress in English as THE MESSAGE: The Bible in Contemporary Language copyright 2002-2003 by Eugene Peterson. All rights reserved.

New Century Version®. (NCV) Copyright © 1987, 1988, 1991 by Word Publishing, a division of Thomas Nelson, Inc. All rights reserved. Used by permission.

The Holy Bible, The Living Bible (TLB), Copyright © 1971 owned by assignment by Illinois Regional Bank N.A. (as trustee). Used by permission of Tyndale House Publishers, Inc., Wheaton, Illinois 60189. All rights reserved.

International Children's Bible®, New Century Version®. (ICB) Copyright © 1986, 1988, 1999 by Tommy Nelson™, a division of Thomas Nelson, Inc. All rights reserved. Used by permission.

The Holy Bible: Revised Standard Version (RSV). Copyright 1946, 1952, 1959, 1973 by the Division of Christian Education of the National Council of the Churches of Christ in the United States of America. All rights reserved. Used by permission.

The New American Standard Bible®, (NASB) Copyright © 1960, 1962, 1963, 1968, 1971, 1972, 1973, 1975, 1977, 1995 by The Lockman Foundation. Used by permission.

The Holman Christian Standard Bible™ (HCSB) Copyright © 1999, 2000, 2001 by Holman Bible Publishers. Used by permission.

Cover Design by Kim Russell / Wahoo Designs
Page Layout by Bart Dawson

ISBN 978-1-60587-428-9

Printed in the United States of America

1 2 3 4 5—QGF—16 15 14 13 12

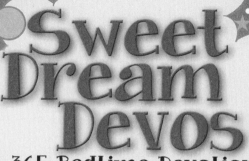

Sweet Dream Devos

365 Bedtime Devotions For Little Girls

A Message to Parents

What do you talk about when you tuck your little girl into bed at night? One of the things you probably talk about—and should talk about—is God's never-ending love for your daughter. And this book of devotionals can help.

Perhaps your daughter's bookshelf is already filled with an interesting, spirit-lifting collection of children's books. If so, that means you're a thoughtful parent who understands the importance of reading to her. And, if you treasure the time you spend reading together during those special moments right before she falls asleep at night, this text will become an important addition to her library.

This book contains 365 brief bedtime devotions, a year's worth of inspiration, wisdom, and assurance. If you have been touched by God's love and His grace, you already know the joy that He has brought into your own life. Now it's your turn to share God's message with the young girl whom He has entrusted to your care. Happy reading! And may God richly bless you and your family now and forever.

DAY 1
Jesus Gives Life

Then Jesus said, "I am the bread that gives life. Whoever comes to me will never be hungry, and whoever believes in me will never be thirsty."

John 6:35 NCV

Who's the best friend any girl has ever had? Who's the best friend the whole wide world has ever had? Jesus, of course! When you invite Him into your heart, Jesus will be your friend, too . . . your friend forever.

Jesus has offered to share the gifts of everlasting life and everlasting love with the world . . . and with you. If you make mistakes, He'll still be your friend. If you behave badly, He'll still love you. If you feel sorry or sad, He can help you feel better.

Jesus wants you to have a happy, healthy life. He wants you to be generous and kind. He wants you to follow His example. The rest is up to you. You can do it! And with a friend like Jesus, you will.

DAY 2
Never-Ending Love

The unfailing love of the Lord never ends!

Lamentations 3:22 NLT

How much does God love you? He loves you so much that He sent His Son Jesus to come to this earth for you! And, when you accept Jesus into your heart, God gives you a gift that is more precious than gold: that gift is called "eternal life" which means that you will live forever with God in heaven!

God's love is bigger and more powerful than anybody can imagine, but it is very real. So do yourself a favor right now: accept God's love with open arms and welcome His Son Jesus into your heart. When you do, your life will be changed today, tomorrow, and forever.

DAY 3
Ending Your Day with God

It is good to give thanks to the Lord, to sing praises to the Most High. It is good to proclaim your unfailing love in the morning, your faithfulness in the evening.

Psalm 92:1-2 NLT

How do you end your day? Are you one of those girls who falls to sleep without saying your prayers, or without thanking God for His blessings? Hopefully not! After all, God loves you very much, and He has given you many gifts. So the right thing to do is to thank Him every night.

Each new day is a gift from God, and every evening gives you another chance to thank Him for that gift. So bedtime is good to spend a few quiet moments thanking the Giver. Saying your prayers is a wonderful way to end your day.

DAY 4
Hopes, Hopes, and More Hopes

Make me hear joy and gladness.

Psalm 51:8 NKJV

Hope is a very good thing to have . . . and to share. So make this promise to yourself and keep it: promise yourself that you'll be a hopeful person. Think good thoughts. Trust God. Become friends with Jesus. And trust your hopes, not your fears. Then, when you've filled your heart with hope and gladness, share your good thoughts with friends. They'll be better for it, and so will you.

DAY 5
It's Easy to Worry

The Lord himself will go before you. He will be with you; he will not leave you or forget you. Don't be afraid and don't worry.

Deuteronomy 31:8 NCV

It's easy to worry about things—big things and little things. But the Bible promises us that if we learn to trust God more and more each day, we won't worry so much.

Are you worried about something? If so, try doing these two things: first, ask God for His help. And second, talk things over with your parents. When you do these things, you won't worry so much. And that's good . . . VERY good!

DAY 6
Asking for Forgiveness

Be even-tempered, content with second place, quick to forgive an offense. Forgive as quickly and completely as the Master forgave you. And regardless of what else you put on, wear love. It's your basic, all-purpose garment. Never be without it.

Colossians 3:13-14 MSG

When you make a mistake or hurt someone's feelings, what should you do? You should say you're sorry and ask for forgiveness. And you should do so sooner, not later.

The longer you wait to apologize, the harder it is on you. So if you've done something wrong, don't be afraid to ask for forgiveness, and don't be afraid to ask for it NOW!

DAY 7
The Courage to Tell the Truth

And you shall know the truth, and the truth shall make you free.

John 8:32 NKJV

Sometimes, we're afraid of what might happen if we tell the truth. Sometimes, instead of doing the courageous thing, we do the unwise thing: we lie.

When we're fearful, we can and should find strength from friends, from family members, and from God.

So if you're afraid to tell the truth, don't be! Keep looking until you find the courage to be honest. Then, you'll discover it's not the truth that you should be afraid of; it's those troublesome, pesky lies!

DAY 8
God Is Faithful

I have set the Lord always before me; because He is at my right hand I shall not be moved.

Psalm 16:8 NKJV

God is faithful. He keeps His promises to us even when we stray far from His will. He continues to love us even when we disobey His commandments. But God does not force His blessings upon us. If we are to experience His love and His grace, we must claim them for ourselves.

Are you discouraged or fearful? Be comforted: God is with you. Are you confused? Listen to the quiet voice of your Heavenly Father. Are you angry? Talk with God and seek His guidance. Are you celebrating a great victory? Thank God and praise Him. He is the Giver of all things good.

DAY 9
Friends Are a Good Thing

If you've gotten anything at all out of following Christ, if his love has made any difference in your life, if being in a community of the Spirit means anything to you, if you have a heart, if you care—then do me a favor: Agree with each other, love each other, be deep-spirited friends.

Philippians 2:1-2 MSG

The Bible tells us that friendship can be a wonderful thing. That's why it's good to know how to make and to keep good friends.

If you want to make lots of friends, practice the Golden Rule with everybody you know. Be kind. Share. Say nice things. Be helpful. When you do, you'll discover that the Golden Rule isn't just a nice way to behave; it's also a great way to make and to keep friends!

Is the Golden Rule Your Rule, Too?

Don't be selfish…. Be humble, thinking of others as better than yourself.

Philippians 2:3 TLB

Is the Golden Rule your rule, or is it just another Bible verse that goes in one ear and out the other? Jesus made Himself perfectly clear: He instructed you to treat other people in the same way that you want to be treated. But sometimes, especially when you're feeling pressure from friends, or when you're tired or upset, obeying the Golden Rule can seem like an impossible task—but it's not. So be kind to everybody and obey God's rule, the Golden Rule, that is.

The Habit of Honesty

Those who want to do right more than anything else are happy. God will fully satisfy them.

Matthew 5:6 ICB

Our lives are made up of lots and lots of habits. And the habits we choose help determine the kind of people we become. If we choose habits that are good, we are happier and healthier. If we choose habits that are bad, then it's too bad for us!

Honesty, like so many other things, is a habit. And it's a habit that is right for you.

Do you want to grow up to become the kind of woman that God intends for you to be? Then get into the habit of being honest with everybody. You'll be glad you did . . . and so will God!

DAY 12
Share Your Blessings

Remember this: the person who sows sparingly will also reap sparingly, and the person who sows generously will also reap generously.

2 Corinthians 9:6 HCSB

Jesus told us that we should be generous with other people, but sometimes we don't feel much like sharing. Instead of sharing the things that we have, we want to keep them all to ourselves. But God doesn't want selfishness to rule our hearts; He wants us to be generous.

Are you lucky enough to have nice things? If so, God's instructions are clear: you must share your blessings with others. And that's exactly the way it should be. After all, think how generous God has been with you.

White Lies?

Doing what is right brings freedom to honest people.

Proverbs 11:6 ICB

Sometimes, people convince themselves that it's okay to tell "little white lies." Sometimes people convince themselves that itsy bitsy lies aren't harmful. But there's a problem: little lies have a way of growing into big ones, and once they grow up, they cause lots of problems.

Remember that lies, no matter what size, are not part of God's plan for our lives, so tell the truth about everything. It's the right thing to do, and besides: when you always tell the truth, you don't have to try and remember what you said!

DAY 14

Obey Your Teachers

And the world with its lust is passing away, but the one who does God's will remains forever.

1 John 2:17 HCSB

It's good to obey your teachers, but before you can obey them, you must make sure you understand what your teachers are saying. So, in order to be an obedient student, you must be a student who knows how to listen.

Once you decide to be a careful listener, you'll become a better learner, too. But if you're determined to talk to other kids while your teachers are teaching, you won't learn very much.

So do yourself a favor: when you go to school or church, listen and obey. You'll be glad you did . . . and your teachers will be glad, too.

DAY 15
No More Tantrums

A patient person [shows] great understanding, but a quick-tempered one promotes foolishness.

Proverbs 14:29 HCSB

Temper tantrums are so silly. And so is pouting. So, of course, is whining. When we lose our tempers, we say things that we shouldn't say, and we do things that we shouldn't do. Too bad!

The Bible tells us that it is foolish to become angry and that it is wise to remain calm. That's why we should learn to control our tempers before our tempers control us.

A Fruitful Friendship

I am the Vine, you are the branches. When you're joined with me and I with you, the relation intimate and organic, the harvest is sure to be abundant.

John 15:5 MSG

Whether you realize it or not, you already have a relationship with Jesus. Hopefully, it's a close relationship! Why? Because the friendship you form with Jesus will help you every day of your life . . . and beyond!

You can either choose to invite Him into your heart, or you can ignore Him altogether. Welcome Him today—and while you're at it, encourage your friends and family members to do the same.

Going to Church

Take heed therefore unto yourselves, and to all the flock, over the which the Holy Ghost hath made you overseers, to feed the church of God.

Acts 20:28 KJV

The Bible teaches that we should worship God in our hearts and in our churches. We have clear instructions to "feed the church of God" and to worship our Creator in the presence of fellow believers.

We have been blessed by God, and we should be faithful to Him. One way that we remain faithful to God is through the practice of regular, purposeful worship with our families. When we worship the Father faithfully and fervently, we are blessed.

DAY 18
Laughter Is a Gift

There is a time for everything, and everything on earth has its special season. There is a time to cry and a time to laugh. There is a time to be sad and a time to dance.

Ecclesiastes 3:1,4 NCV

Do you like to laugh? Of course you do! Laughter is a gift from God that He hopes you'll use in the right way. So here are a few things to remember:

1. God wants you to be happy. 2. Laughter is a good thing when you're laughing at the right things. 3. You should laugh with people, but you should never laugh at them.

God created laughter for a reason...and God knows best. So do yourself a favor: laugh at the right things . . . and laugh a lot!

DAY 19
Be Respectful

Show respect for all people. Love the brothers and sisters of God's family.

1 Peter 2:17 ICB

Are you polite and respectful to your parents and teachers? And do you do your best to treat everybody with the respect they deserve? If you want to obey God's rules, then you should be able to answer yes to these questions.

Remember this: the Bible teaches you to be a respectful person—and if it's right there in the Bible, it's certainly the right thing to do!

DAY 20
Slow Down!

Knowing God leads to self-control. Self-control leads to patient endurance, and patient endurance leads to godliness.

2 Peter 1:6 NLT

Maybe you're one of those girls who try to do everything fast, faster, or fastest! If so, maybe you sometimes do things before you think about the consequences of your actions. If that's the case, it's probably a good idea to slow down a little bit so you can think before you act. When you do, you'll soon discover the value of thinking carefully about things before you get started. And while you're at it, it's probably a good idea to think before you speak, too. After all, you'll never have to apologize for something that you didn't say.

DAY 21
The Words You Speak

If anyone considers himself religious and yet does not keep a tight rein on his tongue, he deceives himself and his religion is worthless.

James 1:26 NIV

The words you speak are important. If you speak kind words, you make other people feel better. And that's exactly what you should do!

How hard is it to say a kind word? Not very! Yet sometimes we're so busy that we forget to say the very things that might make other people feel better.

Kind words help; cruel words hurt. It's as simple as that. And, when we say the right thing at the right time, we give a gift that can change somebody's day or somebody's life.

DAY 22
Trust Him

Trust the Lord with all your heart, and don't depend on your own understanding. Remember the Lord in all you do, and he will give you success.

Proverbs 3:5-6 NCV

Sometimes, things happen that we simply don't understand. But God does. And He has a reason for everything that He does.

God doesn't explain Himself in ways that we can easily comprehend. So here's what we should do: instead of trying to understanding every part of God's unfolding plan for our lives and our world, we must be satisfied to trust Him completely. We cannot know why God does things. We can, however, trust Him, and we should.

DAY 23
Everlasting Protection

The Lord is my rock, my fortress, and my deliverer, my God, my mountain where I seek refuge. My shield, the horn of my salvation, my stronghold, my refuge, and my Savior.

2 Samuel 22:2-3 HCSB

Life isn't always easy. Far from it! Sometimes, life can be very hard indeed. But even when we're upset or hurt, we must remember that we're protected by a loving Heavenly Father.

When we're worried, God can reassure us; when we're sad, God can comfort us. When our feelings are hurt, God is not just near, He is here. We must lift our thoughts and prayers to our Father in heaven. When we do, He will answer our prayers. Why? Because He is our shepherd, and He has promised to protect us now and forever.

DAY 24
Sharing

If you have two shirts, share with the person who does not have one. If you have food, share that too.

Luke 3:11 ICB

How many times have you heard someone say, "Don't touch that; it's mine!" If you're like most of us, you've heard those words many times and you may have even said them yourself.

The Bible tells us that it's better for us to share things than it is to keep them all to ourselves. And the Bible also tells us that when we share, it's best to do so cheerfully. So be sure to share. It's the best way because it's God's way.

DAY 25
Patience and Love

I wait for the Lord; I wait, and put my hope in His word.

Psalm 130:5 HCSB

God has a perfect idea of the kind of people He wants us to become. For starters, He wants us to be loving, kind, and patient—not rude or mean!

The Bible tells us that God is love and that if we wish to know Him, we must have love in our hearts. Sometimes, of course, when we're tired, angry, or frustrated, it is very hard for us to be loving. Thankfully, anger and frustration are feelings that come and go, but God's love lasts forever.

If you'd like to become a more patient girl, talk to God in prayer, listen to what He says, and share His love with your family and friends. God is always listening, and He's ready to talk to you.

DAY 26
Know When to Say No

Wisdom will save you from the ways of wicked men . . . .

Proverbs 2:12 NIV

It happens to all of us at one time or another: a friend asks us to do something that we think is wrong. What should we do? Should we try to please our friend by doing something bad? No way! It's not worth it!

Trying to please our friends is okay. What's not okay is misbehaving in order to do so. Do you have a friend who encourages you to misbehave? Hopefully you don't have any friends like that. But if you do, say "No, NO, NOOOOOO!" And what if your friend threatens to break up the friendship? Let her! Friendships like that just aren't worth it.

DAY 27
When Nobody Is Watching

Moderation is better than muscle, self-control better than political power.

Proverbs 16:32 MSG

When your teachers or parents aren't watching, what should you do? The answer, of course, is that you should behave exactly like you would if they were watching you. But sometimes, you may be tempted to do otherwise.

When a parent steps away or a teacher looks away, you may be tempted to say something or do something that you would not do if they were standing right beside you. But remember this: when nobody's watching, it's up to you to control yourself. That's exactly what everybody wants you to do: your teachers want you to control yourself, and so do your parents. So, by the way, does God.

DAY 28
God's Gifts

Thanks be to God for his indescribable gift!

2 Corinthians 9:15 NIV

All people have special gifts—special blessings from God—and you are no exception. Today, make a promise to yourself that you will earnestly seek to discover the talents that God has given you. Then, keep improving those talents and make them grow. Finally, share your gifts with the world. After all, the best way to say "Thank You" for God's gifts is to use them.

DAY 29
Obeying God

Be gentle with one another, sensitive. Forgive one another as quickly and thoroughly as God in Christ forgave you.

Ephesians 4:32 MSG

How hard is it to forgive people? Sometimes, it's very hard! But God tells us that we must forgive other people, even when we'd rather not forgive them. So, if you're angry with anybody (or if you're upset by something you yourself have done), it's time to forgive.

God instructs us to treat other people exactly as we wish to be treated. When we forgive others, we are obeying our Heavenly Father, and that's exactly what we must try to do.

DAY 30
It Pays to Be Cheerful

Be cheerful. Keep things in good repair. Keep your spirits up. Think in harmony. Be agreeable. Do all that, and the God of love and peace will be with you for sure.

2 Corinthians 13:11 MSG

Few things in life are more sad, or, for that matter, more ridiculous, than a grumpy Christian. Christ promises us a life of abundance and joy, but He does not force His joy upon us. We must claim His joy for ourselves, and when we do, Jesus, in turn, fills our spirits with His power and His love. Then we, as God's children, can share Christ's joy and His message with a world that needs both.

DAY 31
He Answers

For I know the thoughts that I think toward you, says the Lord, thoughts of peace and not of evil, to give you a future and a hope. Then you will call upon Me and go and pray to Me, and I will listen to you.

Jeremiah 29:11-12 NKJV

In case you've been wondering, wonder no more— God does answer your prayers. What God does not do is this: He does not always answer your prayers as soon as you might like, and He does not always answer your prayers by saying "Yes."

God answers prayers not only according to our wishes but also according to His master plan. And guess what? We don't know that plan . . . but we can know the Planner.

Are you praying? Then you can be sure that God is listening. And sometime soon, He'll answer!

DAY 32
Respect for Others

Being respected is more important than having great riches.

Proverbs 22:1 ICB

Do you try to have a respectful attitude towards everybody? Hopefully so!

Should you be respectful of grown ups? Of course. Teachers? Certainly. Family members? Yes. Friends? Yep, but it doesn't stop there. The Bible teaches us to treat all people with respect.

Respect for others is habit-forming: the more you do it, the easier it becomes. So start practicing right now. Say lots of kind words and do lots of kind things, because when it comes to kindness and respect, practice makes perfect.

DAY 33
The Master Teacher

This man came to Him at night and said, "Rabbi, we know that You have come from God as a teacher, for no one could perform these signs You do unless God were with him."

John 3:2 HCSB

Who was the greatest teacher in the history of the world? Jesus was . . . and He still is! Jesus teaches us how to live, how to behave, and how to worship. Now, it's up to each of us, as Christians, to learn the important lessons that Jesus can teach.

Some day soon, you will have learned everything that Jesus has to teach you, right? WRONG!!!!

Jesus will keep teaching you important lessons throughout your life. That's good, because all of us, kids and grown-ups alike, have lots to learn . . . especially from the Master . . . Jesus.

DAY 34
God Wants You to Share

I will make you into a great nation and I will bless you; I will make your name great, and you will be a blessing. I will bless those who bless you, and whoever curses you I will curse; and all peoples on earth will be blessed through you.

Genesis 12:2-3 NIV

You've heard it plenty of times from your parents and teachers: share your things. But it's important to realize that sharing isn't just something that grown-ups want you to do. It's also something that God wants you to do, too.

The word "possessions" is another way of describing the stuff that belongs to you: your clothes, your toys, your books, and things like that are "your possessions."

Jesus says that you should learn how to share your possessions without feeling bad about it. Sometimes, of course, it's very hard to share and very easy to be stingy. But God wants you to share—and to keep sharing! Since that's what God wants, it's what you should want, too.

DAY 35
Real Friends

A friend loves you all the time.

Proverbs 17:17 ICB

The Book of Proverbs tells us that true friends love us always. How wonderful that is! We should thank God for the family and friends He has brought into our lives.

Today, let's give thanks to God for all the people who love us, for brothers and sisters, parents and grandparents, aunts and uncles, cousins, and friends. And then, as a way of thanking God, let's obey Him by being especially kind to our loved ones. They deserve it, and so does He.

DAY 36
Making Things Better

For out of the overflow of the heart the mouth speaks.

Matthew 12:34 NIV

When we're frustrated or tired, it's easier to speak first and think second. But that's not the best way to talk to other people. The Bible tells us that "a good person's words will help many others." But if our words are to be helpful, we must put some thought into them.

If you're tempted to say something unkind, remember your words can and should be helpful to others, not hurtful. God wants to use you to make this world a better place, and He will use the things that you say to help accomplish that goal.

DAY 37
Wisdom from Above

The Lord says, "I will make you wise and show you where to go. I will guide and watch over you."

Psalm 32:8 NCV

Your head is undoubtedly filled with a growing collection of valuable information. But, there is much yet to learn. Wisdom is like a savings account: If you add to it consistently, then eventually you'll have a great sum. The secret to success is consistency.

Would you like to be wise? Then keep learning. Seek wisdom every day, and seek it in the right place. That place, of course, is, first and foremost, the Word of God. It's not enough to simply read God's Word; you've also got to live by it.

Understanding Christ's Love

And I pray that you and all God's holy people will have the power to understand the greatness of Christ's love—how wide and how long and how high and how deep that love is. Christ's love is greater than anyone can ever know, but I pray that you will be able to know that love. Then you can be filled with the fullness of God.

Ephesians 3:18–19 NCV

Christ's love for you is personal. He loves you so much that He gave His life in order that you might spend all eternity with Him. Christ loves you individually and intimately; His is a love unbounded by time or circumstance. Are you willing to experience an intimate relationship with Him? Your Savior is waiting patiently; don't make Him wait a single minute longer. Embrace His love today. Fill yourself with the fullness of God.

DAY 39
God's Power

I pray...that you may know...his uncomparably great power for us who believe....

Ephesians 1:18-19 NIV

How strong is God? Stronger than anybody can imagine! But even if we can't understand God's power, we can respect His power. And we can be sure that God has the strength to guide us and protect us forever.

The next time you're worried or afraid, remember this: if God is powerful enough to create the universe and everything in it, He's also strong enough to take care of you. Now that's a comforting thought!

DAY 40
What Kind of Example?

You are young, but do not let anyone treat you as if you were not important. Be an example to show the believers how they should live. Show them with your words, with the way you live, with your love, with your faith, and with your pure life.

1 Timothy 4:12 ICB

Like it or not, your behavior is a powerful example to others. The question is not whether you will be an example to your friends; the only question is this: What kind of example will you be?

Corrie ten Boom advised, "Don't worry about what you do not understand. Worry about what you do understand in the Bible but do not live by."

And that's good advice because your family and friends are always watching . . . and so, for that matter, is God.

DAY 41
Too Much Stuff

Anyone trusting in his riches will fall, but the righteous will flourish like foliage.

Proverbs 11:28 HCSB

The world is in love with money and the things that money can buy. But, God is not. God cares about people, not possessions, and so should you. So, don't worry about collecting too much stuff. Instead, think about the things you can do to please God. The more you please Him, the happier you'll be.

DAY 42
Sharing and Self-esteem

God loves the person who gives happily.

2 Corinthians 9:7 ICB

Learning how to share can be an important way to build better self-esteem. Why? Because when you learn to share your things, you'll know that you've done exactly what God wants you to do—and you'll feel better about yourself.

The Bible teaches that it's better to be generous than selfish. But sometimes, you won't feel like sharing your things, and you'll be tempted to keep everything for yourself. When you're feeling a little bit stingy, remember this: God wants you to share your things with people who need your help.

When you learn to be a more generous girl, God will be pleased with you . . . and you'll be pleased with yourself.

Obedience

He will teach us of his ways, and we will walk in his paths.

Isaiah 2:3 KJV

It seems like we human beings are constantly getting ourselves into trouble. Why? Because we simply don't take God's instructions to heart.

God has given us a guidebook for life. It's called the Holy Bible, and it contains comprehensive instructions which, if followed, lead to fulfillment, comfort, and abundance. But, if we choose to ignore God's commandments, the results are as predictable as they are unfortunate.

How can you best show your love for the Lord? By obeying Him. And, for further instructions, read the book He wrote.

Be the Right Kind of Christian

The one who plants and the one who waters have the same purpose, and each will be rewarded for his own work.

I Corinthians 3:8 NCV

Do you want to be the kind of Christian that God intends for you to be? It's up to you! You'll be the one who will decide how you behave.

If you decide to obey God and trust His Son, you will be rewarded now and forever. So guard your heart and trust your Heavenly Father. He will never lead you astray.

You Can't Please Everybody

My son, if sinners entice you, don't be persuaded.

Proverbs 1:10 HCSB

Are you one of those girls who tries to please everybody in sight? If so, you'd better watch out!

After all, if you worry too much about pleasing your friends, you may not worry enough about pleasing God.

Whom will you try to please today: your God or your pals? The answer to that question should be simple. Your first job is to obey God's rules . . . and that means obeying your parents, too!

So don't worry too much about pleasing your friends or neighbors. Try, instead, to please your Heavenly Father and your parents. No exceptions.

DAY 46
Do Good Deeds

A good person produces good deeds from a good heart, and an evil person produces evil deeds from an evil heart. Whatever is in your heart determines what you say.

Luke 6:45 NLT

It's good to do good deeds. Even when nobody's watching, God is. And God knows whether you've done the right thing or the wrong thing.

So if you're tempted to misbehave when nobody is looking, remember this: There is never a time when "nobody's watching." Somebody is always watching over you—and that Somebody, of course, is God. Don't let Him down!

DAY 47
Sometimes It's Hard to Be Honest
. . . but It's Always Right

It is better to be poor and honest than to be foolish and tell lies.

Proverbs 19:1 ICB

Telling the truth can be hard sometimes. But even when telling the truth is very hard, that's exactly what you should do. If you're afraid to tell the truth, pray to God for the courage to do the right thing, and then do it!

If you've ever told a big lie, and then had to live with the big consequences of that lie, you know that it's far more trouble to tell a lie than it is to tell the truth. But lies aren't just troubling to us; they're also troubling to God! So tell the truth, even when it's hard to do; you'll be glad you did . . . and so will He!

DAY 48
It's Important to Be Kind

I tell you the truth, anything you did for even the least of my people here, you also did for me.

Matthew 25:40 NCV

The Bible promises that if you're a nice person, good things will happen to you. That's one reason (but not the only reason) that it's important to be kind.

Do you listen to your heart when it tells you to be kind to other people? Hopefully, you do. After all, lots of people in the world aren't as fortunate as you are—and some of these folks are living very near you.

Ask your parents to help you find ways to do nice things for other people. Don't forget that everybody needs love, kindness, and respect, so you should always be ready to share those things.

Parents Can Help

The one who lives with integrity is righteous; his children who come after him will be happy.

Proverbs 20:7 HCSB

Whenever you want to get better at something, you should always be willing to let your parents help out in any way they can. After all, your parents want you to become the very best person you can be. So, if you want to become better at controlling your own behavior, ask your parents to help. How can they help out? By reminding you to slow down and think about things before you do them—not after. It's as simple as that.

Nobody Likes 'Em

Therefore, if anyone is in Christ, he is a new creation; the old has gone, the new has come!

2 Corinthians 5:17 NIV

Mistakes: nobody likes 'em but everybody makes 'em. And you're no different! When you make mistakes (and you will), you should do your best to correct them, to learn from them, and pray for the wisdom to avoid those same mistakes in the future.

If you want to become smarter faster, you'll learn from your mistakes the first time you make them. When you do, that means that you won't keep making the same mistakes over and over again, and that's the smart way to live.

Practicing Forgiveness

Smart people know how to hold their tongue; their grandeur is to forgive and forget.

Proverbs 19:11 MSG

Forgiving other people requires practice and lots of it. So when it comes to forgiveness, here's something you should remember: if at first you don't succeed, don't give up!

Are you having trouble forgiving someone (or, for that matter, forgiving yourself for a mistake that you've made)? If so, remember that forgiveness isn't easy, so keep trying until you get it right . . . and if you keep trying, you can be sure that sooner or later, you will get it right.

DAY 52
Heaven Is Forever

I have told you these things so that in Me you may have peace. In the world you have suffering. But take courage! I have conquered the world.

John 16:33 HCSB

This crazy world can be a place of trouble and danger. Thankfully, God has offered you a permanent home in heaven, a place of unimaginable glory, a place that He has already prepared for you.

In John 16:33, Jesus tells us He has overcome the troubles of this world. We should trust Him, and we should obey His commandments. When we do, we can withstand any problem, knowing that our troubles are only temporary.

DAY 53
Love Yourself, Too!

God began doing a good work in you, and I am sure he will continue it until it is finished when Jesus Christ comes again.

Philippians 1:6 NCV

The Bible teaches you this lesson: you should love everybody—and the word "everybody" includes yourself. Do you treat yourself with honor and respect? You should. After all, God created you in a very special way, and He loves you very much. And if God thinks you are amazing and wonderful, shouldn't you think about yourself in the same way? Of course you should!

So remember this: God wants you to love everybody, including the person you see when you look in the mirror. And one more thing: when you learn how to respect the person in the mirror, you'll be better at respecting other people, too.

DAY 54
Learning How to Share

He that giveth, let him do it with simplicity....

Romans 12:8 KJV

If you're having a little trouble learning how to share your stuff, you're not alone! Most people have problems letting go of things, so don't be discouraged. Just remember that learning to share requires practice and lots of it. The more you share—the more you learn how good it feels—the sooner you'll be able to please God with the generosity and love that flows from your heart.

DAY 55
Sharing Is Better Than Stingy

And God will generously provide all you need. Then you will always have everything you need and plenty left over to share with others.

2 Corinthians 9:8 NLT

The Bible teaches that it's better to be generous than selfish. Sometimes, you won't feel like sharing your things, and you'll be tempted to keep everything for yourself. When you're feeling a little bit stingy, remember this: God wants you to share your things, and He will reward you when you do.

When you learn to be a more generous person, God will be pleased with you . . . and you'll be pleased with yourself. So do yourself (and everybody else) a favor: be a little more generous, starting NOW!

DAY 56
Respecting Other People

Show respect for all people: Love the brothers and sisters of God's family.

I Peter 2:17 NCV

Since you want other people to be kind to you, you should be kind to them. Since you want other people to give you the respect you deserve, you should give them the respect they deserve. Since you want other people to play fair, you should do likewise.

The Golden Rule teaches you to treat other people like you want to be treated. It's a simple rule, and it's simply the right thing to do.

DAY 57
The Blame Game

People's own foolishness ruins their lives, but in their minds they blame the Lord.

Proverbs 19:3 NCV

When something goes wrong, do you look for somebody to blame? And do you try to blame other people even if you're the one who made the mistake? Hopefully not!

It's silly to try to blame other people for your own mistakes, so don't do it.

If you've done something you're ashamed of, don't look for somebody to blame; look for a way to say, "I'm sorry, and I won't make that same mistake again."

Peace at Home

My dear brothers, always be willing to listen and slow to speak. Do not become angry easily. Anger will not help you live a good life as God wants.

James 1:19 ICB

Sometimes, it's easy to become angry with the people we love most, and sometimes it's hard to forgive them. After all, we know that our family will still love us no matter how angry we become. But while it's easy to become angry at home, it's usually wrong.

The next time you're tempted to stay angry at a brother, or a sister, or a parent, remember that these are the people who love you more than anybody else! Then, calm down, and forgive them . . . NOW! Because peace is always beautiful, especially when it's peace at your house.

In the World, but Not of It

In this world you will have trouble. But take heart! I have overcome the world.

John 16:33 NIV

We live in the world, but we should not worship it—yet at every turn, or so it seems, we are tempted to do otherwise. As Warren Wiersbe correctly observed, "Because the world is deceptive, it is dangerous."

The world we live in is a noisy, distracting place, a place that offers countless temptations and dangers. The world seems to cry, "Worship me with your time, your money, your energy, your thoughts, and your life!" But if we are wise, we won't fall prey to that temptation.

C. S. Lewis said, "Aim at heaven and you will get earth thrown in; aim at earth and you will get neither." That's good advice. You're likely to hit what you aim at, so aim high . . . aim at heaven.

Your Attitude

Make your own attitude that of Christ Jesus.

Philippians 2:5 HCSB

What's an attitude? The word "attitude" means "the way that you think." And don't forget this: your attitude is important.

Your attitude can make you happy or sad, grumpy or glad, joyful or mad. And, your attitude doesn't just control the way that you think; it also controls how you behave. If you have a good attitude, you'll behave well. And if you have a bad attitude, you're more likely to misbehave.

Have you spent any time thinking about the way that you think? Do you pay much attention to your attitude? Hopefully so! After all, a good attitude is better than a bad one . . . lots better.

You have more control over your attitude than you think. So do your best to make your attitude a good attitude. One way you can do that is by learning about Jesus and about His attitude toward life. When you do, you'll learn that it's always better to think good thoughts, and it's always better to do good things. Always!

DAY 61
What Your Conscience Says About Forgiveness

Now the goal of our instruction is love from a pure heart, a good conscience, and a sincere faith.

I Timothy 1:5 HCSB

God gave you something called a conscience: it's that little feeling that tells you whether something is right or wrong. Your conscience will usually tell you what to do and when to do it. Trust that feeling.

If you listen to your conscience, it won't be as hard for you to forgive people. Why? Because forgiving other people is the right thing to do. And, it's what God wants you to do. And it's what your conscience tells you to do. So what are you waiting for?

DAY 62
When People Are Cruel

A kind man benefits himself, but a cruel man brings disaster on himself.

Proverbs 11:17 HCSB

Face it: sometimes people can be cruel. And when people are unkind to you or to your friends, you may be tempted to strike back in anger. Don't do it! Instead, remember that God corrects other people's behaviors in His own way, and He doesn't need your help. So even when other people misbehave, God wants you to forgive them . . . and that's what you should do.

DAY 63
Positive Peer Pressure

My dear, dear friends, if God loved us like this, we certainly ought to love each other.

1 John 4:11 MSG

Are your friends the kind of kids who encourage you to behave yourself? If so, you've chosen your friends wisely.

But if your friends try to get you in trouble, perhaps it's time to think long and hard about making some new friends.

Whether you know it or not, you're probably going to behave like your friends behave. So pick out friends who make you want to behave better, not worse. When you do, you'll be saving yourself from a lot of trouble . . . a whole lot of trouble.

DAY 64
How Do They Know?

Do you want to be counted wise, to build a reputation for wisdom? Here's what you do: Live well, live wisely, live humbly. It's the way you live, not the way you talk, that counts.

James 3:13 MSG

How do people know that you're a Christian? Well, you can tell them, of course. And make no mistake about it: talking about your faith in God is a very good thing to do. But simply telling people about Jesus isn't enough. You must also be willing to show people how a real Christian (like you) should behave. Does that sound like a big responsibility? It is . . . but you can do it!

DAY 65
Choosing Wisely

I am offering you life or death, blessings or curses. Now, choose life! . . . To choose life is to love the Lord your God, obey him, and stay close to him.

Deuteronomy 30:19-20 NCV

Choices, choices, choices! You've got so many choices to make, and sometimes, making those choices isn't easy. At times, you're torn between what you want to do and what you ought to do. When that happens, it's up to you to choose wisely . . . or else!

When you make wise choices, you are rewarded; when you make unwise choices, you must accept the consequences. It's as simple as that. So make sure that your choices are pleasing to God . . . or else!

DAY 66
Celebrate!

Celebrate God all day, every day. I mean, revel in him!

Philippians 4:4 MSG

Do you feel like celebrating? Hopefully so! Are you expecting God to do wonderful things? Hopefully so! Are you happy about your family, your friends, and your church? Hopefully so! After all, God loves you, and that fact should make you very happy indeed. So treat every day as a big celebration . . . because that's exactly what every day should be.

DAY 67
The Best Excuse Is No Excuse

Each of us will be rewarded for his own hard work.

I Corinthians 3:8 TLB

What is an excuse? Well, when you make up an excuse, that means that you try to come up with a good reason that you didn't do something that you should have done.

Anybody can make up excuses, and you can too. But you shouldn't get into the habit of making too many excuses. Why? Because excuses

50

don't work. And why don't they work? Because everybody has already heard so many excuses that almost everybody can recognize excuses when they hear them.

So the next time you're tempted to make up an excuse, don't. Instead of making an excuse, do what you think is right. After all, the very best excuse of all . . . is no excuse.

DAY 68
Love to Share

And we have known and believed the love that God has for us. God is love, and he who abides in love abides in God, and God in him.

I John 4:16 NKJV

The Bible tells us that God is love and that if we wish to know Him, we must have love in our hearts. Sometimes, of course, when we're tired, angry, or frustrated, it is very hard for us to be loving. Thankfully, anger and frustration are feelings that come and go, but God's love lasts forever.

If you'd like to improve your day and your life, share God's love with your family and friends. Every time you love, and every time you give, God smiles.

Respecting Others

Just as you want others to do for you, do the same for them.

Luke 6:31 HCSB

How should you treat other people? Jesus has the answer to that question. Jesus wants you to treat other people exactly like you want to be treated: with kindness, respect, and courtesy. When you do, you'll make your family and friends happy . . . and that's what God wants.

So if you're wondering how to treat someone else, follow the Golden Rule: treat the other people like you want them to treat you. When you do, you'll be obeying your Father in heaven and you'll be making other folks happy at the same time.

Setting an Example

Set an example of good works yourself, with integrity and dignity in your teaching.

Titus 2:7 HCSB

The Bible says that you are "the light that gives light to the world." The Bible also says that you should live in a way that lets other people understand what it means to be a good person. And of course, learning to share is an important part of being a good person.

What kind of "light" have you been giving off? Hopefully, you have been a good example for everybody to see. Why? Because the world needs all the light it can get, and that includes your shining light, too!

Every Moment Matters

Lord, tell me when the end will come and how long I will live. Let me know how long I have. You have given me only a short life . . . . Everyone's life is only a breath.

Psalm 39:4–5 NCV

Every day, like every life, is composed of moments. Each moment of your life holds within it the potential to seek God's will and to serve His purposes. If you are wise, you will try to do both.

An important part of wisdom is the wise use of time. How will you invest your time today? Will you savor the moments of your life, or will you squander them? Will you use your time as an instrument of God's will, or will you allow commonplace distractions to rule your day and your life?

The gift of time is a gift from God. Treat it as if it were a precious, fleeting, one-of-a-kind treasure. Because it is.

Feeling Better

A wise person is patient. He will be honored if he ignores a wrong done against him.

Proverbs 19:11 ICB

Is forgiving someone else an easy thing for you to do or a hard thing? If you're like most people, forgiving others can be hard, Hard, HARD! But even if you're having a very hard time forgiving someone, you can do it if you talk things over with your parents, and if you talk things over with God.

Do you find forgiveness difficult? Talk about it and pray about it. You'll feel better when you do.

Solomon Says . . . Be Kind!

A kind person is doing himself a favor. But a cruel person brings trouble upon himself.

Proverbs 11:17 ICB

King Solomon wrote most of the Book of Proverbs; in it, he gave us wonderful advice for living wisely. Solomon warned that unkind behavior leads only to trouble, but kindness is its own reward.

The next time you're tempted to say an unkind word, remember Solomon. He was one of the wisest men who ever lived, and he knew that it's always better to be kind. Now, you know it, too.

DAY 74
Patiently Waiting

We can make our plans, but the LORD determines our steps.

Proverbs 16:9 NLT

God has a plan for you. But God's plan may not always happen in the way that you would like or at the time of your own choosing. Still, God always knows best.

Sometimes, even though you may want something very badly, you must still be patient and wait for the right time to get it, And the right time, of course, is determined by God. So trust Him always, obey Him always, and wait for Him to show you His plans. And that's exactly what He will do.

Changing Habits

Do not be deceived: "Evil company corrupts good habits."

I Corinthians 15:33 NKJV

Most girls have a few habits they'd like to change, and maybe you do, too. If so, God can help.

If you trust God, and if you keep asking Him to help you change bad habits, He will help you make yourself into a new person. So, if at first you don't succeed, keep praying. God is listening, and He's ready to help you become a better person if you ask Him.

Sharing Your Stuff

In every way I've shown you that by laboring like this, it is necessary to help the weak and to keep in mind the words of the Lord Jesus, for He said, "It is more blessed to give than to receive."

Acts 20:35 HCSB

Are you one of those girls who is lucky enough to have a closet filled up with stuff? If so, it's probably time to share some of it.

When your mom or dad says it's time to clean up your closet and give some things away, don't be sad. Instead of whining, think about all the children who could enjoy the things that you don't use very much. And while you're at it, think about what Jesus might tell you to do if He were here. Jesus would tell you to share generously and cheerfully. And that's exactly what you should do!

DAY 77
Following Jesus

Therefore as you have received Christ Jesus the Lord, walk in Him.

Colossians 2:6 HCSB

Since He walked this earth two thousand years ago, Jesus has called upon people of every generation (and that includes you) to follow in His footsteps. And God's Word promises that when you follow in Christ's footsteps, you will experience abundance, happiness, and joy.

God wants you to be a new person through Him. And that's exactly what you should want for yourself, too. God deserves your extreme enthusiasm; the world deserves it; and you deserve the experience of sharing it. So what are you waiting for?

Kindness Starts with You

Be kind to one another, tender-hearted, forgiving each other, just as God in Christ also has forgiven you.

Ephesians 4:32 NASB

If you're waiting for other people to be nice to you before you're nice to them, you've got it backwards. Kindness starts with you! You see, you can never control what other people will say or do, but you can control your own behavior.

The Bible tells us that we should never stop doing good deeds as long as we live. Kindness is God's way, and it should be our way, too.

Always Be Honest

The honest person will live safely, but the one who is dishonest will be caught.

Proverbs 10:9 ICB

Nobody can tell the truth for you. You're the one who decides what you are going to say. You're the one who decides whether your words will be truthful . . . or not.

The word "integrity" means doing the right and honest thing. If you're going to be a person of integrity, it's up to you. If you want to live a life that is pleasing to God and to others, make integrity a habit. When you do, everybody wins, especially you!

Getting to Know Him

If your life honors the name of Jesus, he will honor you.

2 Thessalonians 1:12 MSG

There's really no way around it: If you want to know God, you need to know His Son. And that's good, because getting to know Jesus can—and should—be a wonderful experience.

Jesus has an amazing love for you, so welcome Him into your heart today. When you do, you'll always be grateful that you did.

Making Better Decisions

Don't turn your back on wisdom, for she will protect you. Love her, and she will guard you.

Proverbs 4:6 NLT

How can you make better decisions? A great place to start is by talking things over with God before you spring into action, not after. While you're at it, you can check things out with your parents—or with other concerned adults, like grandparents or teachers. And, you can learn to listen carefully to your conscience.

During the coming year, as you think about the lessons in this book, please take these ideas seriously. When you do, you'll make decisions that will please God and improve your life.

DAY 82
Think Before You Speak

To everything there is a season . . . a time to keep silence, and a time to speak.

Ecclesiastes 3:1,7 KJV

Sometimes, it's easier to say the wrong thing than it is to say the right thing—especially if we're in a hurry to blurt out the first words that come into our heads. But, if we are patient and if we choose our words carefully, we can help other people feel better, and that's exactly what your Heavenly Father wants us to do.

The Book of Proverbs tells us that the right words, spoken at the right time, can be wonderful gifts to our families and to our friends. That's why we should think about the things that we say before we say them, not after. When we do, our words make the world a better place, and that's exactly what God wants!

DAY 83
Time for God

I wait quietly before God, for my hope is in him.

Psalm 62:5 NLT

When it comes to spending time with God, are you a "squeezer" or a "pleaser"? Do you squeeze God into your schedule with a prayer before mealtime, or do you please God by talking to Him far more often than that? If you're wise, you'll form the habit of spending time with God every day.

Even if you're the busiest girl on planet Earth, you can still carve out a little time for God. And when you think about it, isn't that the very least you should do?

DAY 84
Obeying God

But be doers of the word and not hearers only.

James 1:22 HCSB

How can you show God how much you love Him? By obeying His commandments, that's how! When you follow God's rules, you show Him that you have real respect for Him and for His Son.

Sometimes, you will be tempted to disobey God, but don't do it. And sometimes you'll be tempted to disobey your parents or your teachers . . . but don't do that, either.

When your parent steps away or a teacher looks away, it's up to you to control yourself. And of this you can be sure: If you really want to control yourself, you can do it!

DAY 85
Perfect Love

For God so loved the world that he gave his only Son, so that everyone who believes in him will not perish but have eternal life.

John 3:16 NLT

The Bible makes this promise: God is love. It's a big promise, a very important description of what God is and how God works. God's love is perfect. When we open our hearts to His love, we are blessed and we are protected.

Today, offer sincere prayers of thanksgiving to your Heavenly Father. He loves you now and throughout all eternity. Open your heart to His presence and His love.

Finding the Right Friends

As iron sharpens iron, a friend sharpens a friend.

Proverbs 27:17 NLT

Some friends encourage us to obey God—these friends help us make wise choices. Other friends put us in situations where we are tempted to disobey God—these friends tempt us to make unwise choices.

Are you spending time with friends who make you a better Christian? Hopefully so, because one of the best ways to ensure that you follow Christ is to find fellow believers who are willing to follow Him with you.

Be Thankful

Our prayers for you are always spilling over into thanksgivings. We can't quit thanking God our Father and Jesus our Messiah for you!

Colossians 1:3 MSG

Are you a thankful girl? You should be! Whether you realize it or not, you have much to be thankful for. And who has given you all the blessings you enjoy? Your parents are responsible, of course. But all of our blessings really start with God.

All of us should make thanksgiving a habit. Since we have been given so much, the least we can do is say "Thank You" to the One who has given us more blessings than we can possibly ever count.

DAY 88
If You're Trying to Be Perfect

The Lord says, "Forget what happened before, and do not think about the past. Look at the new thing I am going to do. It is already happening. Don't you see it? I will make a road in the desert and rivers in the dry land."

Isaiah 43:18-19 NCV

If you're trying to be perfect, you're trying to do something that's impossible. No matter how much you try, you can't be a perfect person . . . and that's okay.

God doesn't expect you to live a mistake-free life—and neither should you. In the game of life, God expects you to try, but He doesn't always expect you to win. Sometimes, you'll make mistakes, but even then, you shouldn't give up!

So remember this: you don't have to be perfect to be a wonderful person. In fact, you don't even need to be "almost-perfect." You simply must try your best and leave the rest up to God.

DAY 89
Right and Wrong

Lead a tranquil and quiet life in all godliness and dignity.

1 Timothy 2:2 HCSB

If you're old enough to know right from wrong, then you're old enough to do something about it. In other words, you should always try to do the right thing, and you should also do your very best not to do the wrong thing.

The more self-control you have, the easier it is to do the right thing. Why? Because, when you learn to think first and do things next, you avoid lots of silly mistakes. So here's great advice: first, slow down long enough to figure out the right thing to do—and then do it. You'll make yourself happy, and you'll make lots of other people happy, too.

DAY 90
Yes, Jesus Loves You

Just as the Father has loved Me, I also have loved you. Remain in My love.

John 15:9 HCSB

The Bible makes this promise: Jesus loves you. And how should that make you feel? Well, the fact that Jesus loves you should make you very happy indeed, so happy, in fact, that you try your best to do the things that Jesus wants you to do.

Jesus wants you to welcome Him into your heart, He wants to love and obey God, and He wants you to be kind to people. These are all very good things to do . . . and the rest is up to you!

DAY 91
Living in the Spirit of Truth

But when the Spirit of truth comes, he will lead you into all truth.

John 16:13 NCV

God is vitally concerned with truth. His Word teaches the truth; His Spirit reveals the truth; His Son leads us to the truth. When we open our hearts to God, and when we allow Jesus to rule over our thoughts and our lives, God reveals Himself, and we come to understand the truth about ourselves and the Truth about God's gift of grace.

The familiar words of John 8:32 remind us that "you shall know the truth, and the truth shall make you free" (NKJV). May we, as believers, seek God's truth and live by it, this day and forever.

How Would He Behave?

And he saith unto them, follow me, and I will make you fishers of men. And they straightway left their nets, and followed him.

Matthew 4:19-20 KJV

If Jesus were here, how would He behave? He would be loving and forgiving. He would worship God with sincere devotion. He would serve other people, and He would always abide by the Golden Rule. If Jesus were here, He would stand up for truth and speak out against evil.

We read in the Bible that Jesus wants each of us to do our best to be like Him. We can't be perfect Christians, but we can do our best to obey God's commandments and to follow Christ's example. When we do so, we bring honor to the One who gave His life for each of us.

DAY 93
A Pleasing Attitude

Set your minds on what is above, not on what is on the earth.

Colossians 3:2 HCSB

God knows everything about you, including your attitude. And when your attitude is good, God is pleased . . . very pleased.

Are you interested in pleasing God? Are you interested in pleasing your parents? Your teachers? And your friends? If so, try to make your attitude the best it can be. When you try hard to have a good attitude, you'll make other people feel better—and you'll make yourself feel better, too.

DAY 94
Your Continual Feast

A cheerful heart has a continual feast.

Proverbs 15:15 HCSB

What is a continual feast? It's a little bit like a non-stop birthday party: fun, fun, and more fun! The Bible tells us that a cheerful heart can make life like a continual feast, and that's something worth working for.

Where does cheerfulness begin? It begins inside each of us; it begins in the heart. So please be thankful to God for His blessings, and let's show our thanks by sharing good cheer wherever we go. This old world needs all the cheering up it can get . . . and so do we!

Your Most Important Book

But grow in the grace and knowledge of our Lord and Savior Jesus Christ. To Him be the glory both now and forever. Amen.

2 Peter 3:18 NKJV

What book contains everything that God has to say about His rules and His Son? The Bible, of course. If you read the Bible every day, you'll soon learn how God wants you to behave.

Since doing the right thing (and the smart thing) is important to God, it should be important to you, too. And you'll learn what's right by reading the Bible.

The Bible is the most important book you'll ever own. It's God's Holy Word. Read it every day, and follow its instructions. When you do, you'll be safe now and forever.

DAY 96
Slowing Down for God!

Don't burn out; keep yourselves fueled and aflame. Be alert servants of the Master, cheerfully expectant. Don't quit in hard times; pray all the harder.

Romans 12:11-12 MSG

Everybody knows you're a very busy girl. But here's a question: are you able to squeeze time into your schedule for God? Hopefully so!

Nothing is more important than the time you spend with your Heavenly Father. So take some time tonight and every night to pray and to thank God for His blessings. God will be glad you did, and you'll be glad, too.

DAY 97
Keep the Peace

Love must be without hypocrisy. Detest evil; cling to what is good. Show family affection to one another with brotherly love. Outdo one another in showing honor.

Romans 12:9–10 HCSB

Sometimes, it's easiest to become angry with the people we love the most. After all, we know that they'll still love us no matter how angry we become. But while it's easy to become angry at home, it's usually wrong.

The next time you're tempted to become angry with a brother, or a sister, or a parent, remember that these are the people who love you more than anybody else! Then, calm down. Because peace is always beautiful, especially when it's peace at your house.

DAY 98
God's House

For where two or three are gathered together in My name, I am there among them.

Matthew 18:20 HCSB

When your parents take you to church, are you pleased to go? Hopefully so. After all, church is a wonderful place to learn about God's rules.

The church belongs to God just as surely as you belong to God. That's why the church is a good place to learn about God and about His Son Jesus.

So when your mom and dad take you to church, remember this: church is a fine place to be . . . and you're lucky to be there.

DAY 99
Moving On

Mockers can get a whole town agitated, but those who are wise will calm anger.

Proverbs 29:8 NLT

Are you the kind of girl who is kind to everybody? Hopefully so!

Tomorrow, and every day after that, make sure that you're a person who is known for the kind way that you treat everybody. That's how God wants you to behave.

And if someone says something to you that isn't very nice, don't pay too much attention. Just forgive that person as quickly as you can, and try to move on . . . as quickly as you can.

DAY 100
Becoming a More Patient Person

Be gentle to all, able to teach, patient.

2 Timothy 2:24 NKJV

The Book of Proverbs tells us that patience is a very good thing. But for most of us, patience can also be a very hard thing. After all, we have many things that we want, and we want them NOW!

But the Bible tells us that we must learn to wait patiently for the things that God has in store.

Are you having trouble being patient? If so, remember that patience takes practice, and lots of it, so keep trying. And if you make a mistake, don't be too upset. After all, if you're going to be a really patient person, you shouldn't just be patient with others, you should also be patient with yourself.

He Can Take Care of Our Problems

Do not love the world or the things that belong to the world. If anyone loves the world, love for the Father is not in him.

1 John 2:15 HCSB

An old hymn contains the words, "This world is not my home; I'm just passing through." Thank goodness! This crazy world can be a place of trouble and danger. Thankfully, your real home is heaven, a place where you can live forever with Jesus.

In John 16:33, Jesus tells us He has overcome the troubles of this world. We should trust Him, and we should obey His commandments. When we do, we are forever blessed by the Son of God and His Father in heaven.

DAY 102
Prized Possessions

Whoever does not care for his own relatives, especially his own family members, has turned against the faith and is worse than someone who does not believe in God.

I Timothy 5:8 NCV

Your most prized earthly possession is not your cool new toy or a video game or anything you can buy. Your most prized earthly possession is, of course, your family. Your family is a priceless gift from God. Treasure it, protect it, and dedicate it to Him. When you place God at the center of your family, He will bless your family forever.

DAY 103
God's Love

For the Lord is good. His unfailing love continues forever, and his faithfulness continues to each generation.

Psalm 100:5 NLT

God is a loving Father. We are God's children, and we are called upon to be faithful to Him. We return our Father's love by sharing it with others.

We honor our Heavenly Father by obeying His commandments and sharing His message. When we do, we are blessed . . . and the Father smiles.

Kind Thoughts

Whoever forgives someone's sin makes a friend, but gossiping about the sin breaks up friendships.

Proverbs 17:9 NCV

What does it mean to forgive? Forgiveness means that you decide to change your angry thoughts into kind thoughts. Forgiveness means that you decide not to stay mad at somebody who has done something wrong. Forgiveness happens when you decide that obeying God is more important than staying angry.

Sometimes forgiveness can be very hard, but it's the right thing to do. Why? Because forgiveness is God's way, and you should make it your way, too!

Forgiveness Can Be Hard

Anyone who claims to live in God's light and hates a brother or sister is still in the dark.

1 John 2:9 MSG

But God tells us that we must forgive other people, even when we'd rather not. So, if you're angry with anybody (or if you're upset by something you yourself have done), it's time to forgive . . . now!

But what if you have already tried to forgive somebody yet simply can't do it? Then you must keep trying. If you can't seem to forgive someone, you should keep asking God to help you until you do. And you can be sure of this: if you keep asking for God's help, He will give it.

DAY 106
Everybody Makes Mistakes

Instead, God has chosen the world's foolish things to shame the wise, and God has chosen the world's weak things to shame the strong.

I Corinthians 1:27 HCSB

Do you make mistakes? Of course you do . . . everybody does. When you make a mistake, you must try your best to learn from it so that you won't make the very same mistake again. And, if you have hurt someone—or if you have disobeyed God—you must ask for forgiveness.

Remember: mistakes are a part of life, but the biggest mistake you can make is to keep making the same mistake over and over and over again.

DAY 107
Your Family Is a Gift

Love must be without hypocrisy. Detest evil; cling to what is good. Show family affection to one another with brotherly love. Outdo one another in showing honor.

Romans 12:9–10 HCSB

Your family is a wonderful, one-of-a-kind gift from God. And your family members love you very much—what a blessing it is to be loved!

Have you ever really stopped to think about how much you are loved? Your parents love you (of course) and so does everybody else in your family. But it doesn't stop there. You're also an important part of God's family . . . and He loves you more than you can imagine.

What should you do about all the love that comes your way? You should accept it; you should be thankful for it; and you should share it.

DAY 108
Don't Copy Friends Who Misbehave

Stay away from a foolish man; you will gain no knowledge from his speech.

Proverbs 14:7 HCSB

If your friends misbehave, do you misbehave right along with them, or do you tell them to stop? Usually, it's much easier to go along with your friends, even if you know they're misbehaving. But it's always better to do the right thing, even if it's hard.

Sometimes, grownups must stand up for the things they believe in. When they do, it can be hard for them, too. But the Bible tells us over and over again that we should do the right thing, not the easy thing.

When your friends misbehave, it can spoil everything. So if your friends behave badly, don't copy them! And if your friends keep behaving badly, choose different friends.

DAY 109
Learning to Control Yourself

But endurance must do its complete work, so that you may be mature and complete, lacking nothing.

James 1:4 HCSB

If you're having trouble learning how to control your actions or your emotions, you're not alone! Most people have problems with self-control from time to time, so don't be discouraged. Just remember that self-control requires practice and lots of it. So if you're a little discouraged, don't give up. Just keep working on improving your self-control until you get better at it. . . . and if you keep trying, you can be sure that sooner or later, you will get better at it.

DAY 110
What Happens When You Pray

Rejoice always! Pray constantly. Give thanks in everything, for this is God's will for you in Christ Jesus.

1 Thessalonians 5:16-18 HCSB

Prayer changes things, and it changes you. When you pray, good things happen, so pray often. Don't wait for bedtime to pray; find time to pray throughout the day. Even open-eyed prayers work, and God is always listening.

So pray.

DAY 111
Patience and Peace

I leave you peace. My peace I give you. I do not give it to you as the world does. So don't let your hearts be troubled.

John 14:27 ICB

Patience and peace go together. And the words from John 14:27 remind us that Jesus offers us peace, not as the world gives, but as He alone gives. We, as believers, can accept His peace or ignore it. When we accept the peace of Jesus Christ into our hearts, our lives are changed forever, and we become more loving, patient Christians.

Christ's peace is offered freely; it has already been paid for; it is ours for the asking. So let us ask . . . and then share.

DAY 112
Staying Out of Trouble

Don't envy bad people; don't even want to be around them. All they think about is causing a disturbance; all they talk about is making trouble.

Proverbs 24:1-2 MSG

One way that you can feel better about yourself is by staying out of trouble. And one way that you can stay out of trouble is by making friends with people who, like you, want to do what's right.

Are your friends the kind of kids who encourage you to behave yourself? If so, you've chosen your friends wisely. But if your friends try to get you in trouble, perhaps it's time to think long and hard about making some new friends.

Whether you know it or not, you're probably going to behave like your friends behave. So pick out friends who make you want to behave better, not worse. When you do, you'll feel better about yourself . . . a whole lot better.

DAY 113
Yes, Jesus Loves You!

You're blessed when you're content with just who you are—no more, no less. That's the moment you find yourselves proud owners of everything that can't be bought.

Matthew 5:5 MSG

Have you heard the song "Jesus Loves Me"? Probably so. It's a happy song that should remind you of this fact: Jesus loves you very much.

When you invite Jesus into your heart, He'll protect you forever. If you have problems, He'll help you solve them. When you aren't perfect, He'll still love you. If you feel sorry or sad, He can help you feel better.

Yes, Jesus loves you . . . and you should love yourself. So the next time you feel sad about yourself . . . or something that you've done . . . remember that Jesus loves you, your family loves you, and you should feel that way, too.

The Very Best Time to Forgive Somebody Is Now

Working together with Him, we also appeal to you: "Don't receive God's grace in vain." For He says: In an acceptable time, I heard you, and in the day of salvation, I helped you. Look, now is the acceptable time; look, now is the day of salvation.

2 Corinthians 6:1-2 HCSB

When is the best time to forgive somebody? Well, as the old saying goes, there's no time like the present. So if you have somebody you need to forgive, why not forgive that person today?

Forgiving other people is one of the ways that we make ourselves feel better. So if you're still angry about something that somebody did, forgive that person right now. There is no better time.

Friends Should Share

The righteous give without sparing.

Proverbs 21:26 NIV

How can you be a good friend? One way is by sharing. And here are some of the things you can share: smiles, kind words, pats on the back, your toys, school supplies, books, and, of course, your prayers.

Would you like to make your friends happy? And would you like to make yourself happy at the same time? Here's how: treat your friends like you want to be treated. That means obeying the Golden Rule, which means sharing. In fact, the more you share, the better friend you'll be.

DAY 116
Let's Be Patient

Knowledge begins with respect for the Lord, but fools hate wisdom and self-control.

Proverbs 1:7 NCV

The Bible tells us that we should be patient with everybody, not just with parents, teachers, and friends. In the eyes of God, all people are very important, so we should treat them that way.

Of course it's easy to be nice to the people we want to impress, but what about everybody else? Jesus gave us clear instructions: He said that when we do a good deed for someone less fortunate than we are, we have also done a good deed for our Savior. And as Christians, that's exactly what we are supposed to do!

Martha and Mary

But Martha was pulled away by all she had to do in the kitchen. Later, she stepped in, interrupting them. "Master, don't you care that my sister has abandoned the kitchen to me? Tell her to lend me a hand." The Master said, "Martha, dear Martha, you're fussing far too much and getting yourself worked up over nothing. One thing only is essential, and Mary has chosen it—it's the main course, and won't be taken from her."

Luke 10:40-42 MSG

Okay, after that rather long Bible passage, your devotional is almost up, so we'll make it short and sweet: Martha was concerned with doing things for Jesus. Mary was concerned with being with Jesus. Mary made the better choice. Why? Because we need to be with Christ before we start doing things for Him. End of lesson.

Avoiding Mischief

Therefore as you have received Christ Jesus the Lord, walk in Him.

Colossians 2:6 HCSB

Face facts: not everybody you know is well behaved. Your first job is to recognize bad behavior when you see it . . . and your second job is to make sure that you don't join in!

The moment that you decide to avoid mischief whenever you see it is the moment that you'll make yourself happy, your parents happy, and God happy . . . and you'll stay out of trouble.

DAY 119
The Wisdom of Thanksgiving

Give thanks to the Lord, for He is good; His faithful love endures forever.

Psalm 106:1 HCSB

God's Word makes it clear: a wise heart is a thankful heart. Period. We are to worship God, in part, by the genuine gratitude we feel in our hearts for the marvelous blessings that He has bestowed upon us. Yet even the most saintly among us must endure periods of sadness, fear, and doubt. Why? Because we are imperfect people who are incapable of perfect gratitude. Still, we must seek to cleanse our hearts of negative emotions and fill them, instead, with praise, love, hope, and thanksgiving. To do otherwise is to be unfair to ourselves, to our loved ones, and to our God.

Think About the Other Person

I pray that your love for each other will overflow more and more, and that you will keep on growing in your knowledge and understanding.

Philippians 1:9 NLT

There's an old saying that goes something like this: "Try to put yourself in the other person's shoes." It means that the more you understand somebody, the easier it is to forgive that person.

When you become angry with someone, try putting yourself in the other person's shoes. When you do, perhaps you'll be a little bit more understanding—and a little bit quicker to forgive.

Loving God, Loving People

Jesus replied, "'Love the Lord your God with all your heart and with all your soul and with all your mind.' This is the first and greatest commandment. And the second is like it: 'Love your neighbor as yourself.' All the Law and the Prophets hang on these two commandments."

Matthew 22:37-40 NIV

Christ's words are clear: He instructs us to love the Lord with all our hearts and to love our neighbors as we love ourselves. The Golden Rule is the perfect rule to use when you're trying to figure out how to treat somebody else. By the way, when you are kind and good, you bring honor to the Son of God who, in His infinite wisdom, made love His greatest commandment.

DAY 122
Being a Good Example to Your Friends

We have around us many people whose lives tell us what faith means. So let us run the race that is before us and never give up. We should remove from our lives anything that would get in the way and the sin that so easily holds us back.

Hebrews 12:1 NCV

Are you a girl whose behavior serves as a good example for other kids? If so, congratulations! God smiles upon people (like you) who do what's right, but that's not all. God also rewards good behavior when He sees it (and you can be sure that He does see it!).

So do yourself and your friends a favor: Do the right thing every chance you get.

DAY 123
Make Them Proud

Give generously, for your gifts will return to you later.

Ecclesiastes 11:1 NLT

It's tempting to be selfish, but it's wrong. It's tempting to want to keep everything for yourself, but it's better to share. It's tempting to say, "No, that's MINE!" but it's better to say, "I'll share it with you."

Are you sometimes tempted to be a little stingy? Are you sometimes tempted to say, "No, I don't want to share that!"—and then do you feel a little sorry that you said it? If that describes you, don't worry: everybody is tempted to be a little bit selfish. Your job is to remember this: even when it's tempting to be selfish, you should try very hard not to be. Because when you're generous, not selfish, you'll make your parents proud and you'll make your Father in Heaven proud, too.

DAY 124
About Barnabas

Barnabas was a good man, full of the Holy Spirit and full of faith.

Acts 11:23-24 ICB

Barnabas was a leader in the early Christian church who was known for his kindness and for his ability to encourage others. Because of Barnabas, many people were introduced to Christ.

We become like Barnabas when we speak kind words to our families and to our friends. And then, because we have been generous and kind, the people around us can see how Christians should behave. So when in doubt, be kind and generous to others, just like Barnabas.

DAY 125
Willing to Forgive

Talk and act like a person expecting to be judged by the Rule that sets us free. For if you refuse to act kindly, you can hardly expect to be treated kindly. Kind mercy wins over harsh judgment every time.

James 2:12-13 MSG

The Bible tells us this: When other people do things that are wrong, we should forgive them. God's Word also tells us that when we're willing to forgive others, God is quick to forgive us for the mistakes that we make.

Has somebody done something that makes you angry? Talk things over with your mom or dad, and then be ready to forgive the person who has hurt your feelings. And remember: God wants you to hurry up and forgive others, just like God is always in a hurry to forgive you.

DAY 126
A Wise King

If you need wisdom—if you want to know what God wants you to do—ask him, and he will gladly tell you. He will not resent your asking.

James 1:5 NLT

Solomon wasn't just a king. He was also a very wise man and a very good writer. He even wrote several books in the Bible! So when he finally put down his pen, what was this wise man's final advice? It's simple: Solomon said: "Honor God and obey His commandments."

The next time you have an important choice to make, ask yourself this: "Am I honoring God and obeying Him? And am I doing what God wants me to do?" If you can answer those questions with a great big "YES," then go ahead. But if you're uncertain if the choice you are about to make is the right one, slow down. Why? Because that's what Solomon says . . . and that's what God says, too!

Working Together

Work at getting along with each other and with God. Otherwise you'll never get so much as a glimpse of God.

Hebrews 12:14 MSG

Helping other people can be fun! When you help others, you feel better about yourself—and you'll know that God approves of what you're doing.

When you learn how to cooperate with your family and friends, you'll soon discover that it's more fun when everybody works together.

So do everybody a favor: learn better ways to share and better ways to cooperate. It's the right thing to do.

Difficult Days

We take the good days from God—why not also the bad days?

Job 2:10 MSG

Face it: some days are better than others. But even on the days when you don't feel very good, God never leaves you for even a moment. So if you need assistance, you can always pray to God, knowing that He will listen and help.

If you're feeling unhappy, talk things over with God, and while you're at it, be sure and talk things over with your parents, too. And remember this: the sooner you start talking, the sooner things will get better.

Good Friends Behave

As iron sharpens iron, so people can improve each other.

Proverbs 27:17 NCV

Our world is filled with pressures: some good, some bad. The pressures that we feel to follow God's rules are the good kind of pressures (and the friends who make us want to obey God are good friends). But sometimes, we may feel pressure to misbehave, pressure from friends who want us to disobey the rules.

If you want to please God and your parents, make friends with people who behave themselves. When you do, you'll be much more likely to behave yourself, too . . . and that's a very good thing.

DAY 130
Good and Evil

Friend, don't go along with evil. Model the good. The person who does good does God's work. The person who does evil falsifies God, doesn't know the first thing about God.

3 John 1:11 MSG

When other people are unkind, you may be tempted to strike back in anger. But God doesn't want you to fight your way through life! God wants you to forgive other people, even when they haven't behaved themselves, even when they've been very mean. So, when other people aren't nice, forgive them as quickly as you can. And let God take care of everything else.

DAY 131
Forgive and Forget

And forgive us our sins, for we ourselves also forgive everyone in debt to us.

Luke 11:4 HCSB

Have you heard the saying, "Forgive and forget"? Well, it's certainly easier said than done. It's easy to talk about forgiving somebody, but actually forgiving that person can be much harder to do. And when it comes to forgetting, forget about it!

Sometimes, it's impossible to forget the people who hurt our feelings. But even if we can't forget, we can forgive. And that's exactly what God teaches us to do.

DAY 132
An Honest Heart

In every way be an example of doing good deeds. When you teach, do it with honesty and seriousness.
Titus 2:7 NCV

Where does honesty begin? In your own heart and your own head. If you sincerely want to be an honest person, then you must ask God to help you find the courage and the determination to be honest all of the time.

Honesty is not a "sometimes" thing. If you intend to be a truthful person, you must make truthfulness a habit that becomes so much a part of you that you don't have to decide whether or not you're going to tell the truth. Instead, you will simply tell the truth because it's the kind of person you are.

Lying is an easy habit to fall into, and a terrible one. So make up your mind that you're going to be an honest person, and then stick to your decision. That's what your parents want you to do, and that's what God wants, too. Since they love you more than you know, trust them.

DAY 133
God Is Close-by

Fear not, for I am with you; Be not dismayed, for I am your God. I will strengthen you.

Isaiah 41:10 NKJV

Here's a promise you can depend on: wherever you are, God is always there, too.

God doesn't take vacations, and He doesn't play hide-and-seek. He's always "right here, right now," waiting to hear from you. So if you're wondering where God is, wonder no more. He's here. And that's a promise!

DAY 134
Lost in the Crowd?

We must obey God rather than men.

Acts 5:29 HCSB

Rick Warren observed, "Those who follow the crowd usually get lost in it." We know those words to be true, but oftentimes we fail to live by them. Instead of trusting God for guidance, we imitate our friends and suffer the consequences.

Instead of getting lost in the crowd, you should find guidance from your parents and from God. When you do, you'll be happier . . . much happier!

DAY 135
God's Protection

God's solid foundation stands firm.

2 Timothy 2:19 HCSB

The Bible makes this promise: God will care for you and protect you. In the 6th chapter of Matthew, Jesus made this point clear when He said,

Do not worry about your life, what you will eat or what you will drink; nor about your body, what you will put on. Is not life more than food and the body more than clothing? Look at the birds of the air, for they neither sow nor reap nor gather into barns; yet your heavenly Father feeds them. Are you not of more value than they? Which of you by worrying can add one cubit to his stature? . . . Therefore do not worry about tomorrow, for tomorrow will worry about its own things. Sufficient for the day is its own trouble (25-27, 34 NKJV).

This beautiful passage reminds you that God still sits in His heaven and you are His beloved child. Simply put, you are protected.

DAY 136
You'll Feel Better About Yourself

So don't get tired of doing what is good. Don't get discouraged and give up, for we will reap a harvest of blessing at the appropriate time.

Galatians 6:9 NLT

The Bible teaches us to treat other people with respect, kindness, courtesy, and love. When we do, we make other people happy, we make God happy, and we feel better about ourselves, too.

So if you're wondering how to make the world—and your world—a better place, here's a great place to start: let the Golden Rule be your rule. When you do, you'll like yourself a little better . . . and so will other people.

DAY 137
Today's Happiness

But happy are those . . . whose hope is in the LORD their God.

Psalm 146:5 NLT

If we could decide to be happy "once and for all," life would be so much simpler, but it doesn't seem to work that way. If we want happiness to last, we need to create good thoughts every day that we live. Yesterday's good thoughts don't count . . . we've got to think more good thoughts now.

Each new day is a gift from God, so treat it that way. Think about it like this: today is another wonderful chance to celebrate God's gifts.

So celebrate—starting now—and keep celebrating forever!

DAY 138
God's Friendship

Greater love has no one than this, that he lay down his life for his friends.

John 15:13 NIV

There's an old song that says, "What a friend we have in Jesus." Those words are certainly true! When you invite Him into your heart, Jesus will be your friend tonight, tomorrow, and forever.

Jesus wants you to have a happy, healthy life. He wants you to behave yourself, and He wants you to take care of yourself. And now, it's up to you to do your best to live up to the hopes and dreams of your very best friend: Jesus.

You're Not Expected to Be Perfect

If we confess our sins to him, he is faithful and just to forgive us and to cleanse us from every wrong.

1 John 1:9 NLT

When you make a mistake, do you get really mad at yourself . . . or maybe really, really, really mad? Hopefully not! After all, everybody makes mistakes, and nobody is expected to be perfect. Even when you make mistakes, God loves you . . . so you should love yourself, too.

So the next time you make a mistake, learn from it. And after you've learned your lesson, try never to make that same mistake again. But don't be too hard on yourself. God doesn't expect you to be perfect, and since He loves you anyway, you should feel that way, too.

The Stuff You Own Isn't as Important as You May Think

Don't be obsessed with getting more material things. Be relaxed with what you have.

Hebrews 13:5 MSG

Here's something to remember about stuff: It's not that important!

Lots of people are in love with money and the things that money can buy. God is not. God cares about people, not possessions, and so must you.

You should not be too concerned about the clothes you wear, or the things you own. And above all, don't ever let your self-esteem depend upon the things that you (or your parents) own.

The stuff that you own isn't nearly as important as the love that you feel in your heart—love for your family, love for your friends, and love for your Father in heaven.

DAY 141
It's a Good Feeling to Obey and Forgive

This is love for God: to obey his commands.

1 John 5:3 NIV

We know that it's right to forgive other people and wrong to stay angry with them. But sometimes, it's so much easier to do the wrong thing than it is to do the right thing, especially when we're tired or frustrated.

When you do the right thing by forgiving other people, you'll feel good because you'll know that you're obeying God. And that's a very good feeling indeed. So make this promise to yourself and keep it: play by the rules—God's rules. You'll always be glad you did.

DAY 142
Share the Good News

Christ did not send me to baptize people but to preach the Good News. And he sent me to preach the Good News without using words of human wisdom so that the cross of Christ would not lose its power.

I Corinthians 1:17 NCV

A good way to build your faith is by talking about it—and that's what God wants you to do.

In his second letter to Timothy, Paul shares a message to believers of every generation when he writes, "God has not given us a spirit of timidity" (1:7). Paul's meaning is clear: When you share your testimony, you must be courageous and unashamed.

You live in a world that desperately needs the healing message of Jesus Christ. Every believer, including you, bears responsibility for sharing the Good News. It is important to remember that you give your testimony through your words and your actions.

Don't Give Up!

So we must not get tired of doing good, for we will reap at the proper time if we don't give up.

Galatians 6:9 HCSB

Occasional disappointments are simply a fact of life. But when we encounter these hardships, we should never lose faith.

Are you willing to keep going even when you meet unexpected troubles? If you decide to work your way through temporary setbacks, you may soon be surprised at the creative ways God finds to help determined people like you—people who possess the wisdom, the faith, and the courage to persevere.

Look Ahead

Learn the truth and never reject it. Get wisdom, self-control, and understanding.

Proverbs 23:23 NCV

Maybe you've heard this old saying: "Look before you leap." What does that saying mean? It means that you should stop and think before you do something. Otherwise, you might be sorry you did it.

Your parents are trying to teach you how to slow down and make better decisions. Why? Because your parents want what's best for you, that's why!

So here's something that you can do: think about the consequences of your behaviors before you do something silly or dangerous . . . or both.

DAY 145
It Pays to Praise

Is anyone happy? Let him sing songs of praise.

James 5:13 NIV

The Bible makes it clear: it pays to say "thank You" to God. But sometimes, we may not feel like thanking anybody, not even our Father in heaven. If we ever stop praising God, it's a big mistake . . . a VERY BIG mistake.

When you stop to think about it, God has been very generous with you . . . and He deserves a great big "thanks" for all those amazing gifts.

Do you want an attitude that pleases God? Then make sure that your attitude praises God. And don't just praise Him on Sunday morning. Praise Him every day, starting with this one.

Be Patient

But reject foolish and ignorant disputes, knowing that they breed quarrels. The Lord's slave must not quarrel, but must be gentle to everyone, able to teach, and patient.

2 Timothy 2:23-24 HCSB

If you've lost patience with someone, or if you're angry, take a deep breath and then ask yourself a simple question: "How would Jesus behave if He were here?" The answer to that question will tell you what to do.

Jesus was quick to speak kind words, and He was quick to forgive others. We must do our best to be like Him. When we do, we will be patient, loving, understanding, and kind.

Start Sharing Now

Never walk away from someone who deserves help; your hand is God's hand for that person.

Proverbs 3:27 MSG

When is the best time to share? Whenever you can—and that means right now, if possible.

When you start thinking about the things you can share, you probably think mostly about things that belong to you (like toys or clothes), but there are many more things you can share (like love, kindness, encouragement, and prayers). That means you have the opportunity to share something with somebody almost any time you want. And that's exactly what God wants you to do—so start sharing now and don't ever stop.

DAY 148
Keep Learning About Self-Control

For the Son of man shall come in the glory of his Father with his angels; and then he shall reward every man according to his works.

Matthew 16:27 KJV

Who needs to learn more about self-control? You do! Why? Well, for one thing, you'll discover that good things happen to girls (like you) who are wise enough to think ahead and smart enough to look before they leap.

Whether you're at home or at school, you'll learn that the best rewards go to the kids who control their behavior—not to the people who let their behaviors control them!

Please God First

So let us come boldly to the throne of our gracious God. There we will receive his mercy, and we will find grace to help us when we need it.

Hebrews 4:16 NLT

Please don't worry too much about pleasing other people. You should try to please God, not people. The expectations that matter are God's expectations, pure and simple. And everything else should take a back seat.

So, do your best to please God, and don't worry too much about what other people think. And, when it comes to meeting the unrealistic expectations of our crazy world, forget about trying to meet those unrealistic expectations and concentrate, instead, on living a life that's pleasing to God.

God Is Watching

Remember that those who do good prove that they are God's children, and those who do evil prove that they do not know God.

3 John 1:11 NLT

Even when nobody's watching, God is. And He knows whether you've done the right thing or the wrong thing. So if you're tempted to misbehave when nobody is looking, remember this: There is never a time when "nobody's watching." Somebody is always watching over you—and that Somebody, of course, is your Father in Heaven. Don't let Him down!

DAY 151
Your Family Has Rules

This is how we are sure that we have come to know Him: by keeping His commands.

1 John 2:3 HCSB

Face facts: your family has rules . . . rules that you're not supposed to break. If you're old enough to know right from wrong, then you're old enough to do something about it. In other words, you should always try to obey your family's rules.

How can you tell "the right thing" from "the wrong thing"? By listening carefully to your parents, that's how.

The more self-control you have, the easier it is to obey your parents. Why? Because, when you learn to think first and do things next, you avoid making silly mistakes. So here's what you should do: First, slow down long enough to listen to your parents. Then, do the things that you know your parents want you to do.

The Good in Others, and You

Dear friend, do not imitate what is evil, but what is good. The one who does good is of God; the one who does evil has not seen God.

3 John 1:11 HCSB

If you look for the good in other people, you'll probably find it. And, if you look for the good things in life, you'll probably find them, too.

But if spend your time looking for things that aren't so good, you'll most certainly find plenty of bad things to look at. So what should you do? It's simple: you should look for the good things.

When you start looking for good things, you'll find them everywhere: in church, at school, in your neighborhood, and at home.

So don't waste your time on things that make you feel angry, discouraged, worried, guilty, or afraid. Look, instead, for the good things in life, the things that your Heavenly Father wants you to pay attention to.

DAY 153
The Right Choice

But Daniel purposed in his heart that he would not defile himself. . . .

Daniel 1:8 KJV

Your life is a series of choices. From the instant you wake up in the morning until the moment you nod off to sleep at night, you make lots of decisions: decisions about the things you do, decisions about the words you speak, and decisions about the thoughts you choose to think.

So, if you want to lead a life that is pleasing to God, you must make choices that are pleasing to Him. He deserves no less . . . and neither, for that matter, do you.

DAY 154
The Rich Harvest

Now this I say, he who sows sparingly will also reap sparingly, and he who sows bountifully will also reap bountifully.

2 Corinthians 9:6 NASB

How can we serve God? By sharing His message and His love with those who cross our paths.

Everywhere we look, or so it seems, the needs are great. And at every turn, it seems, so are the temptations. Still, our challenge is clear: we must love God, obey His commandments, trust His Son, and serve His children. When we place the Lord in His rightful place—at the center of our lives—we will reap a bountiful spiritual harvest that will endure forever.

DAY 155
Love People Who Are Hard to Love

You have heard it said, "Love your neighbor and hate your enemy." But I tell you: Love your enemies and pray for those who persecute you, that you may be sons of your Father in heaven.

Matthew 5:43-45 NIV

Sometimes people can be rude . . . very rude. You will face countless opportunities to lose your temper when other folks behave badly. But God has a better plan: He wants you to forgive people and move on. Remember that God has already forgiven you, so it's only right that you should be willing to forgive others.

So here's some good advice: Forgive everybody as quickly as you can, and leave the rest up to God.

Quiet Charity

Be careful not to do your acts of righteousness before men, to be seen by them. If you do, you will have no reward from your Father in heaven.

Matthew 6:1 NIV

Hymn writer Fanny Crosby wrote, "To God be the glory; great thing He hath done!" But sometimes, because we are imperfect human beings, we seek the glory. Sometimes, when we do good deeds, we seek to glorify our achievements in a vain attempt to build ourselves up in the eyes of our neighbors. To do so is a profound mistake.

God's Word gives specific instructions about how we should approach our acts of charity: The glory must go to God, not to us. All praise belongs to the Giver of all good gifts: our Father in Heaven. We are simply people sharing His generosity, and we must remain humble . . . extremely humble.

His Joy, Our Joy

I've told you these things for a purpose: that my joy might be your joy, and your joy wholly mature.

John 15:11 MSG

Christ made it clear to His followers: He intended that His joy would become their joy. And it's still true today: Christ intends that His believers share His love with His joy in their hearts. Yet sometimes, amid the inevitable hustle and bustle of life, we can lose—at least for a while—the joy of Christ as we wrestle with the challenges of daily living.

C. H. Spurgeon, the 19th-century English clergyman, advised, "The Lord is glad to open the gate to every knocking soul. It opens very freely. Have faith and enter at this moment through holy courage. If you knock with a heavy heart, you shall yet sing with joy of spirit. Never be discouraged!"

DAY 158
Your Picture

For God so loved the world that he gave his only Son, so that everyone who believes in him will not perish but have eternal life.

John 3:16 NLT

If God had a refrigerator in heaven, your picture would be on it! And that fact should make you feel very good about the person you are and the person you can become.

God's love for you is bigger and more wonderful than you can imagine, So do this, and do it right now: accept God's love with open arms and welcome His Son Jesus into your heart. When you do, you'll feel better about yourself . . . and your life will be changed forever.

What's Really Important

A pretentious, showy life is an empty life; a plain and simple life is a full life.

Proverbs 13:7 MSG

"So much stuff to shop for, and so little time . . ." These words describe lots of people, but please don't let those words describe you!

The Bible teaches this important lesson: it's not good to be too concerned about money or the stuff that money can buy. So don't worry too much about the things you can buy in stores. Worry more about obeying your parents and obeying your Heavenly Father—that's what's really important.

Listening Quietly and Carefully

A wise man will hear and increase in learning, and a man of understanding will acquire wise counsel.

Proverbs 1:5 NASB

Have you learned how to sit quietly and listen to your parents and your teachers? Have you learned how to listen respectfully—with your ears open wide and your mouth closed tight? If so, give yourself a big pat on the back (or if you can't reach way back there, ask your mom or dad to do it for you!).

An important part of learning self-control is learning how to be quiet when you're supposed to be quiet. It isn't always easy, but the sooner you learn how to sit quietly and behave respectfully, the better. So you might as well start today.

DAY 161
Jesus Offers Peace

I have told you these things, so that in me you may have peace. In this world you will have trouble. But take heart! I have overcome the world.

John 16:33 NIV

Jesus offers us peace . . . peace in our hearts and peace in our homes. But He doesn't force us to enjoy His peace—we can either accept His peace or not.

When we accept the peace of Jesus Christ by opening up our hearts to Him, we feel much better about ourselves, our families, and our lives.

Would you like to feel a little better about yourself and a little better about your corner of the world? Then open up your heart to Jesus, because that's where real peace begins.

DAY 162
How Much Is Too Much?

Since we entered the world penniless and will leave it penniless, if we have bread on the table and shoes on our feet, that's enough.

1 Timothy 6:7-8 MSG

How much stuff is too much stuff? Well, if your desire for stuff is getting in the way of your desire to know God, then you've got too much stuff—it's as simple as that.

If you find yourself worrying too much about stuff, it's time to change the way you think about the things you own. Stuff isn't really very important to God, and it shouldn't be too important to you.

DAY 163
Be Responsible

So then each of us shall give account of himself to God.

Romans 14:12 NKJV

Nobody can be patient for you. You've got to be patient for yourself. Certainly your parents can teach you about patience, but when it comes to controlling your temper, nobody can control it for you; you've got to control it yourself.

In the Book of Galatians, Paul writes, "We must not tire of doing good." And that's an important lesson: even when we're tired or frustrated, we must do our best to do the right thing.

So the next time you're tempted to lose your temper, stop for a moment and remember that when it comes to good deeds and good behavior, it's all up to you.

DAY 164
Nobody's Perfect

For everything created by God is good, and nothing should be rejected if it is received with thanksgiving.
I Timothy 4:4 HCSB

Face facts: nobody's perfect . . . not even you! And remember this: it's perfectly okay not to be perfect. In fact, God doesn't expect you to be perfect, and you shouldn't expect yourself to be perfect, either.

Are you one of those people who can't stand to make a mistake? Do you think that you must please everybody all the time? If so, here's some advice: DON'T BE SO HARD ON YOURSELF! Mistakes happen . . . and besides, if you learn something from your mistakes, you'll become a better person.

DAY 165
Obedience Is a Choice

Those who obey his commands live in him, and he in them. And this is how we know that he lives in us: We know it by the Spirit he gave us.

1 John 3:24 NIV

You have a choice to make: are you going to be an obedient girl or not? Remember: the decision to be obedient—or the decision not to be obedient—is a decision that you must make for yourself.

If you decide to behave yourself you've made a smart choice. If you decide to obey your parents, you've made another smart choice. If you decide to pay attention to your teachers, you've made yet another wise choice. BUT . . . if you decide not to be obedient, you've made a silly choice.

What kind of person will you choose to be? An obedient, well-behaved person or the opposite? Before you answer that question, here's something to think about: obedience pays . . . and disobedience doesn't.

DAY 166
He Is Everywhere

God did this so that men would seek him and perhaps reach out for him and find him, though he is not far from each one of us.

Acts 17:27 NIV

God is everywhere you have ever been. And He is everywhere you will ever go. That's why you can speak to God any time you need to.

If you are afraid or discouraged, you can turn to God for strength. If you are worried, you can trust God's promises. And if you are happy, you can thank Him for His gifts.

God is right here, and so are you. And He's waiting patiently to hear from you, so why not have a word with Him right now?

DAY 167
When God Speaks Quietly

Speak, Lord. I am your servant and I am listening.

1 Samuel 3:10 NCV

Sometimes God speaks loudly and clearly. More often, He speaks in a quiet voice—and if you are wise, you will be listening carefully when He does.

To do so, you must carve out quiet moments each day to study His Word and sense His direction.

Can you be quiet long enough to listen to your conscience? And are you willing to pray sincerely and then to wait quietly for God's response. Hopefully so. Usually God refrains from sending His messages on stone tablets or city billboards. More often, He communicates in quieter ways. If you really desire to hear His voice, you must listen carefully, and you must do so in the silent corners of your quiet, willing heart.

DAY 168
Each Day Is a Gift

How happy are those who can live in your house, always singing your praises. How happy are those who are strong in the Lord . . . .

Psalm 84:4-5 NLT

God wants you to have a happy, joyful life. But that doesn't mean that you'll be happy all the time. Sometimes, you won't feel like feeling happy, and when you don't, your attitude won't be very good.

When you're feeling a little tired or sad, here's something to remember: This day is a gift from God. And it's up to you to enjoy this day by trying to be cheerful, helpful, courteous, and well behaved. How can you do these things? A good place to start is by doing your best to think good thoughts.

DAY 169
Get Over It

Do not remember the past events, pay no attention to things of old. Look, I am about to do something new; even now it is coming. Do you not see it? Indeed, I will make a way in the wilderness, rivers in the desert.

Isaiah 43:18-19 HCSB

An important part of learning how to forgive is learning how to get over the things that happened yesterday. What happened yesterday is past. And, if what happened yesterday has made you unhappy, today is as good a day as any to start getting over your hurt feelings.

Are you still angry with someone? Has that person said she was sorry and tried to make things better? If so, talk to your parents about it! They'll help you understand that you can't change the past, but you can get over it.

DAY 170
A Royal Law

This royal law is found in the Scriptures: "Love your neighbor as yourself." If you obey this law, then you are doing right.

James was the brother of Jesus and a leader of the early Christian church. In a letter that is now a part of the New Testament, James reminded his friends of a "royal law." That law is the Golden Rule.

When we treat others in the same way that we wish to be treated, we are doing the right thing. James knew it and so, of course did his brother Jesus. Now we should learn the same lesson: it's nice to be nice; it's good to be good; and it's great to be kind.

DAY 171
You're So Very Special

Blessed is the man who does not condemn himself.

Romans 14:22 HCSB

When God made you, He made you in a very special way. In fact, you're a wonderful, one-of-a-kind creation, a special person unlike any other.

Do you realize how special you are? Do you know that God loves you because of who you are (not because of the things you've done)? And do you know that God has important things for you to do? Well whether you realize it or not, all these things are all true.

So the next time you feel bad about something you've done, take a look in the mirror, and remember that you're looking at a wonderfully special person . . . you!

God loves you; your parents love you; your family loves you . . . and that's the way that you should feel about yourself, too.

DAY 172
Keep Growing Up

Therefore, leaving the elementary message about the Messiah, let us go on to maturity.

Hebrews 6:1 HCSB

When will you be completely grown up? Hopefully never! God has a way of helping you continue to grow as a Christian throughout your entire life if you continue to worship Him.

If you learn about God's Word and talk to Him through your prayers, He has much to teach you, so keep learning about God. And never stop.

Do the Right Thing: Share!

It is well with the man who deals generously and lends.

Psalm 112:5 RSV

It's a fact: sharing makes you a better person. Why? Because when you share, you're doing several things: first, you're obeying God; and, you're making your corner of the world a better place; and you're learning exactly what it feels like to be a generous, loving person.

When you share, you have the fun of knowing that your good deeds are making other people happy. When you share, you're learning how to become a better person. When you share, you're making things better for other people and for yourself. So do the right thing: share!

Keeping a Thankful Attitude

And whatever you do, in word or in deed, do everything in the name of the Lord Jesus, giving thanks to God the Father through Him.

Colossians 3:17 HCSB

Do you have a thankful attitude? Hopefully so! After all, you've got plenty of things to be thankful for. Even during those times when you're angry or tired, you're a very lucky person.

Who has given you all the blessings you enjoy? Your parents are responsible, of course. But all of your blessings really start with God. That's why you should say "Thank You" to God many times each day. He's given you so much.

DAY 175
Waiting Your Turn

Don't be impatient for the Lord to act! Travel steadily along his path. He will honor you....

Psalm 37:34 NLT

When we're standing in line or waiting our turn, it's tempting to scream, "Me first!" It's tempting, but it's the wrong thing to do! The Bible tells us that we shouldn't push ahead of other people; instead, we should do the right thing—and the polite thing—by saying, "You first!"

Sometimes, waiting your turn can be hard, especially if you're excited or in a hurry. But even then, waiting patiently is the right thing to do. Why? Because parents say so, teachers say so, and, most importantly, God says so!

DAY 176
Truth Matters

He has showed you, O man, what is good. And what does the LORD require of you? To act justly and to love mercy and to walk humbly with your God.

Micah 6:8 NIV

If you're tempted to say something that isn't true, stop and ask yourself a simple question: "How would Jesus behave if He were here?" The answer to that question will tell you what to say.

Jesus told His followers that the truth would make them free. As believers, we must do our best to know the truth and to tell it. When we do, we behave as our Savior behaved, and that's exactly how God wants us to behave.

DAY 177
Count Your Blessings

Enter his gates with thanksgiving; go into his courts with praise. Give thanks to him and bless his name. For the Lord is good. His unfailing love continues forever, and his faithfulness continues to each generation.

Psalm 100:4-5 NLT

If you sat down and began counting your blessings, how long would it take? A very, very long time! Your blessings include your life, your family, your friends, your talents, and possessions, for starters. But, your greatest blessing—a gift that is yours for the asking—is God's gift of eternal life through Christ Jesus.

You can never count up every single blessing that God has given you, but it doesn't hurt to try . . . so get ready, get set, go—start counting your blessings RIGHT NOW!

DAY 178
Prayerful Hearts and Willing Hands

So you may walk in the way of goodness, and keep to the paths of righteousness. For the upright will dwell in the land, and the blameless will remain in it.

Proverbs 2:20-21 NKJV

The old saying is both familiar and true: We must pray as if everything depended upon God, but work as if everything depended upon us. Yet sometimes, when we are tired or discouraged, we may allow our worries to sap our energy and our hope. God has other intentions. God intends that we pray for things, and He intends that we be willing to work for the things that we pray for. More importantly, God intends that our work should become His work.

DAY 179
Obedience Leads to Happiness

You are young, but do not let anyone treat you as if you were not important. Be an example to show the believers how they should live. Show them with your words, with the way you live, with your love, with your faith, and with your pure life.

1 Timothy 4:12 ICB

Do you want to be happy? Then you should learn to obey your parents and your teachers. And, of course, you should also learn to obey God. When you do, you'll discover that happiness goes hand-in-hand with good behavior.

The happiest people do not misbehave; the happiest people are not cruel or greedy. The happiest people don't disobey their parents, their teachers, or their Father in heaven. The happiest people are those who obey the rules . . .

And it's up to you to make sure that you're one of those happy people.

DAY 180
Stop and Think

Now you must rid yourselves of all such things as these: anger, rage, malice . . . .

Colossians 3:8 NIV

When we lose control of our emotions, we do things that we shouldn't do. Sometimes, we throw tantrums. How silly! Other times we pout or whine. Too bad!

The Bible tells us that it is foolish to become angry and that it is wise to remain calm. That's why we should learn to slow down and think about things before we do them.

Do you want to make life better for yourself and for your family? Then be patient and think things through. Stop and think before you do things, not after. It's the wise thing to do.

DAY 181
The World's Best Friend

Jesus Christ is the same yesterday, today, and forever.

Hebrews 13:8 HCSB

Who's the best friend this world has ever had? Jesus, of course. And when you form a life-changing relationship with Him, He'll be your best friend, too . . . your friend forever.

Jesus wants you to enjoy a happy, healthy life. He wants you to walk with Him and to share His Good News. You can do it. And with a friend like Jesus, you will.

DAY 182
Our Problems =
God's Opportunities

As for God, his way is perfect. All the LORD's promises prove true. He is a shield for all who look to him for protection.

Psalm 18:30 NLT

Here's a riddle: What is it that is too unimportant to pray about yet too big for God to handle? The answer, of course, is: "nothing."

What we see as problems God sees as opportunities. And if we are to trust Him completely, we must admit that even when our own vision is dreadfully limited, His vision is perfect. So, the next time you have a problem, remember that God may be trying to teach you an important lesson. He may be trying to teach you to trust Him completely.

DAY 183
God Wrote a Book

For I am not ashamed of the gospel, because it is God's power for salvation to everyone who believes.

Romans 1:16 HCSB

If you want to know God, you should read the book He wrote. It's called the Bible (of course!), and God uses it to teach you and guide you. The Bible is not like any other book. It is an amazing gift from your Heavenly Father.

D. L. Moody observed, "The Bible was not given to increase our knowledge but to change our lives." God's Holy Word is, indeed, a life-changing, one-of-a-kind treasure. Handle it with care, but more importantly, handle it every day!

DAY 184
Life Is a Gift

Live full lives, full in the fullness of God. God can do anything, you know—far more than you could ever imagine or guess or request in your wildest dreams! He does it not by pushing us around but by working within us, his Spirit deeply and gently within us.

Ephesians 3:19-20 MSG

Life is a gift from God. A wonderful gift; a glorious and amazing gift. Your job is to unwrap that gift, to use it wisely, and to give thanks to the Giver.

Are you going to treat this day (and every one hereafter) as a special gift to be enjoyed and celebrated? You should—and if you really want to please God, that's exactly what you will do.

Inside Out

God does not see the same way people see. People look at the outside of a person, but the Lord looks at the heart.

I Samuel 16:7 NCV

Other people see you from the outside, and sometimes people will judge you by the way you look. But God doesn't care how you look on the outside. Why? Because God is wiser than that; God cares about what you are on the inside—God sees your heart.

If you're like most people, you'll worry a little bit about the way you look (or maybe you worry a lot about it). But please don't worry too much about your appearance!

How you look on the outside isn't important . . . but how you feel on the inside is important. So don't worry about trying to impress other people. Instead of trying to impress other kids, try to impress God by being the best person you can be.

Be Still

Knowing God leads to self-control. Self-control leads to patient endurance, and patient endurance leads to godliness.

2 Peter 1:6 NLT

Sometimes it's hard to sit still, and sometimes it's even harder to be patient! So here's something worth remembering: God wants us to be patient, and we must obey Him or suffer the consequences.

We should be patient with our families, with our friends, and with ourselves . . . especially with ourselves.

You Don't Have to Be Perfect

You're blessed when you're content with just who you are—no more, no less. That's the moment you find yourselves proud owners of everything that can't be bought.

Matthew 5:5 MSG

When God made you, He gave you special talents and opportunities that are yours and yours alone. That means you're a very special, one-of-a-kind person, but that doesn't mean that you should expect to be perfect. After all, only one earthly being ever lived life to perfection, and He was, of course, Jesus. And Jesus loves you even when you're not perfect. Your parents feel the same way. And if all those people love you, you should love yourself, too.

DAY 188
Need More Patience?
Pray About It!

For the eyes of the Lord are over the righteous, and his ears are open unto their prayers: but the face of the Lord is against them that do evil.

1 Peter 3:12 KJV

Would you like to become a more patient person? Then pray about it. Would you like to learn how to use better self-control? Then pray about it. Are you tempted to throw a temper tantrum? Pray about it.

Whenever you pray about something, God hears your prayer . . . and He can help. So don't worry about things; pray about them. God is waiting . . . and listening!

DAY 189
Pleasing God

Unless the Lord builds a house, the work of the builders is useless.

Psalm 127:1 NLT

Do you want to please God and receive His blessings? Then obey Him. When you're faced with a hard choice, slow down and think about what you're about to do. Then, try your hardest to obey your parents and your Creator. When you do, you will be blessed today, and tomorrow, and forever.

DAY 190
Thinking About Your Thoughts

Set your minds on what is above, not on what is on the earth.

Colossians 3:2 HCSB

Do you try to think about things that are good, true, and pleasing to God? The Bible says that you should. Do you lift your hopes and your prayers to God many times each day? The Bible says that you should. Do you turn away from bad thoughts and bad people? The Bible says that you should.

The Bible instructs you to guard your thoughts against things that are hurtful or wrong. And when you turn away from the bad and turn instead toward God and His Son Jesus, you will be protected and you will be blessed.

Patience Pays

A patient spirit is better than a proud spirit.

Ecclesiastes 7:8 HCSB

Do you need help becoming a more patient person? If so, ask God; He's always ready, willing, and able to help. In fact, the Bible promises that when we sincerely seek God's help, He will give us the things we need.

So, if you want to become a better person, bow your head and start praying about it. And then rest assured that with God's help, you can change for the better . . . and you will!

Sharing with Your Family

A person who gives to others will get richer. Whoever helps others will himself be helped.

Proverbs 11:25 ICB

A good place to start sharing is at home—but it isn't always an easy place to start. Sometimes, especially when we're tired or mad, we don't treat our family members as nicely as we should. And that's too bad!

Do you have brothers and sisters? Or cousins? If so, you're lucky.

Sharing your things—without whining or complaining—is a wonderful way to show your family that you love them. So the next time a brother or sister or cousin asks to borrow something, say "yes" without getting mad. It's a great way to say, "I love you."

DAY 193
Don't Judge!

Don't pick on people, jump on their failures, criticize their faults—unless, of course, you want the same treatment. That critical spirit has a way of boomeranging.

Matthew 7:1-2 MSG

Here's something worth thinking about: If you judge other people harshly, God will judge you in the same way. But that's not all (thank goodness!). The Bible also promises that if you forgive other people, you, too, will be forgiven.

Are you tempted to blame people, criticize people, or judge people? If so, remember this: God is already judging what people do, and He doesn't need—or want—your help.

Beyond Anger

Mockers can get a whole town agitated, but those who are wise will calm anger.

Proverbs 29:8 NLT

Your temper is either your master or your servant. Either you control it, or it controls you. And the extent to which you allow anger to rule your life will determine, to a surprising extent, the quality of your relationships with others and your relationship with God.

Anger and peace cannot coexist in the same mind. So obey God's Word by turning away from anger today and every day. You'll be glad you did, and so will your family and friends.

Obeying Your Parents

We must obey God rather than men.

Acts 5:29 NASB

When your parents ask you to do something, do you usually obey them or do you usually ignore them? When your parents try to get your attention, do you listen or not? When your parents make rules, do you obey those rules or do you break them? Hopefully, you've learned to listen to your parents and to obey.

In order to be an obedient person, you must first learn how to control yourself—otherwise, you won't be able to behave yourself even if you want to. Controlling yourself means that you must slow down long enough to listen to your parents, and then you must be willing to do something about the things your parents tell you to do.

When you learn the importance of obedience, you'll soon discover that good things happen when you behave yourself. And the sooner you learn to listen and to obey, the sooner those good things will start happening . . . to you!

DAY 196
Your Amazing Talents!

Now there are varieties of gifts, but the same Spirit. And there are varieties of ministries, and the same Lord.

I Corinthians 12:4-5 NASB

Face facts: you've got very special talents, talents that have been given to you by God. So here's a question: will you use your talents or not? God wants you to use your talents to become a better person and a better Christian. And that's what you should want for yourself.

As you're trying to figure out exactly what you're good at, be sure and talk about it with your parents. They can help you decide how best to use and improve the gifts God has given you.

DAY 197
Lessons You Can Learn

Remember what you are taught. And listen carefully to words of knowledge.

Proverbs 23:12 ICB

You can learn a lot about life by paying attention to the things that happen around you . . . and that's exactly what God wants you to do. God is trying to teach you things, and you can learn those things the easy way (by paying attention and obeying God's rules) or the hard way (by making the same mistakes over and over again until you finally learn something from them). Of course, it's better to learn things sooner rather than later . . . starting now.

DAY 198
The Gold Standard

Therefore, whatever you want others to do for you, do also the same for them—this is the Law and the Prophets.

Matthew 7:12 HCSB

The words of Matthew 7:12 remind us that, as believers in Christ, we should treat others as we wish to be treated. This is called the Golden Rule, but for Christians, it's worth much more than gold.

Do you want other people to forgive you when you make mistakes? Of course you do. And that's why you should be willing to forgive them.

The Golden Rule should be your tool for deciding how you will treat others. So use the Golden Rule as your guide for living and forgiving!

DAY 199
Real Faith

But whoever keeps His word, truly in him the love of God is perfected. This is how we know we are in Him: the one who says he remains in Him should walk just as He walked.

I John 2:5-6 HCSB

Jesus wants to have a real relationship with you. Are you willing to have a real friendship with Him? Unless you can answer this question with a resounding "Yes," you may miss out on some wonderful things.

Every day offers yet another opportunity to behave yourself like a real Christian. When you do, God will guide your steps and bless your endeavors . . . forever.

DAY 200
Choices Matter

The thing you should want most is God's kingdom and doing what God wants. Then all these other things you need will be given to you.

Matthew 6:33 NCV

There's really no way to get around it: choices matter. If you make good choices, good things will usually happen to you. And if you make bad choices, bad things will usually happen.

The next time you have an important choice to make, ask yourself this: "Am I doing what God wants me to do?" If you can answer that question with a great big "YES," then go ahead. But if you're not sure if the choice you are about to make is right, slow down. Because choices matter a lot!

Always the Right Thing to Do

Tell each other the truth because we all belong to each other . . . .

Ephesians 4:25 ICB

It's important to be honest. When you tell the truth, you'll feel better about yourself, and other people will feel better about you, too. But that's not all. When you tell the truth, God knows—and He will reward you for your honesty.

Telling the truth is hard sometimes. But it's better to be honest, even when it's hard. So remember this: telling the truth is always the right thing to do . . . always.

Friends You Can Trust

Friends come and friends go, but a true friend sticks by you like family.

Proverbs 18:24 MSG

All lasting friendships are built upon both honesty and trust. Without trust, friends soon drift apart. But with trust, friends can stay friends for a lifetime.

As Christians, we should always try to be trustworthy friends. And, we should be thankful for the people who are loyal friends to us. When we treat other people with honesty and respect, we not only make more friends, but we also keep the friendships we've already made.

Do you want friends you can trust? Then start by being a friend they can trust. That's the way to make your friendships strong, stronger, and strongest!

Keep On Forgiving

You have heard that it was said, "Love your neighbor and hate your enemies." But I say to you, love your enemies. Pray for those who hurt you.

Matthew 5:43–44 NCV

If you forgive somebody once, that's enough, right? WRONG!!! Even if you've forgiven somebody many times before, you must keep on forgiving.

Jesus teaches us that we must keep forgiving people even if they continue to misbehave. Why? Because we, too, need to be forgiven over and over again. And if God keeps forgiving us, then we must be willing to do the same thing for others.

Room to Grow

So let us stop going over the basics of Christianity again and again. Let us go on instead and become mature in our understanding.

Hebrews 6:1 NLT

Even if you're very mature for your age, you've still got lots of room to grow.

The 19th-century writer Hannah Whitall Smith observed, "The maturity of a Christian experience cannot be reached in a moment." No kidding. In truth, the search for spiritual growth lasts a lifetime.

No Secrets

The eyes of the Lord are in every place, keeping watch . . . .

Proverbs 15:3 NKJV

Even when nobody else is watching, God is. Nothing that we say or do escapes the watchful eye of our Lord. God understands that we are not perfect, but He also wants us to live according to His rules, not our own.

The next time that you're tempted to say something that you shouldn't say or to do something that you shouldn't do, remember that you can't keep secrets from God. So don't even try!

When to Stop Temper Tantrums

A hot-tempered person starts fights and gets into all kinds of sin.

Proverbs 29:22 NLT

Temper tantrums are one of the silliest ways to lose self-control. Why? Because when we lose our temper, we say things that we shouldn't say, and we do things that we shouldn't do. And to make matters worse, once the tantrum is over, we usually feel embarrassed or worse.

The Bible tells us that it isn't very smart to become angry. That's why we should learn to stop temper tantrums before they get started.

Wisdom Is as Wisdom Does

A foolish person enjoys doing wrong, but a person with understanding enjoys doing what is wise.

Proverbs 10:23 NCV

Wisdom, like so many other things in life, is far easier to articulate than it is to demonstrate. In other words, it is far easier to talk about wisdom than it is to live wisely.

Do you sincerely seek to become wise? Then you must find ways to transform your wise thoughts into wise behaviors. And until you do, you may walk and talk wisely, but you will not really be wise.

DAY 208
Being a Good Samaritan

Never walk away from someone who deserves help; your hand is God's hand for that person.

Proverbs 3:27 MSG

Sometimes we would like to help make the world a better place, but we're not sure how to do it. Jesus told the story of the "Good Samaritan," a man who helped a fellow traveler when no one else would. We, too, should be good Samaritans when we find people who need our help. A good place to start helping other people is at home. And of course, we should also offer our help at school and at church.

Another way that we can help other people is to pray for them. God always hears our prayers, so we should talk with Him as often as we can. When we do, we're not only doing a wonderful thing for the people we pray for, we're also doing a wonderful thing for ourselves, too. Why? Because we feel better about ourselves when we're helping other people. And the more we help others, the better we should feel about ourselves.

DAY 209
Be Kind

So rid yourselves of all wickedness, all deceit, hypocrisy, envy, and all slander.

I Peter 2:1 HCSB

Do you know what gossip is? It's when we say bad things about people who are not around. When we gossip, we hurt others and we hurt ourselves. That's why the Bible tells us that gossip is wrong.

Sometimes, it's tempting to say bad things about people, and when we do, it makes us feel important . . . for a while. But, after a while, the bad things that we say come back to hurt us, and of course they hurt other people, too.

So if you want to be a kind person and a good friend, don't gossip . . . and don't listen to people who do.

Look Before You Leap

Enthusiasm without knowledge is not good. If you act too quickly, you might make a mistake.

Proverbs 19:2 NCV

Are you sometimes just a little bit impulsive? Do you sometimes fail to look before you leap? If so, God wants you to be a little bit more careful—or maybe a lot more careful!

The Bible makes it clear: we're supposed to behave wisely, not carelessly. But sometimes we're tempted to rush ahead and do things before we think about them.

So do yourself a big favor—slow down, think things through, and look carefully before you leap.

Only One You

To acquire wisdom is to love oneself; people who cherish understanding will prosper.

Proverbs 19:8 NLT

How many girls in the world are exactly like you? Only one—the girl you see every time you look in the mirror. In other words, the only person in the world who's exactly like you . . . IS YOU! And that means you're special: special to God, special to your family, special to your friends, and a special addition to God's wonderful world!

The Bible says that God made you in "an amazing and wonderful way." So the next time that you start feeling like you don't measure up, remember this: when God made all the people of the earth, He only made one you. And that means you're a V.I.P. And what is a V.I.P.?

A "Very Important Person," of course.

DAY 212
Use Your Ears!

My dearly loved brothers, understand this: everyone must be quick to hear, slow to speak, and slow to anger.

James 1:19 HCSB

When God made you, He gave you two ears and one mouth for a very good reason: you can learn at least twice as much by listening as you can by talking. That's why it's usually better to listen first and talk second. But when you're frustrated or tired, it's easy to speak first and think later.

A big part of growing up is learning how to slow down long enough to listen to the things that people have to say. So the next time you're tempted to turn off your ears and tune up your mouth, stop, listen, and think. After all, God gave you two wonderful ears for a very good reason: to use them.

DAY 213
If You Think You Can

Though a righteous man falls seven times, he will get up, but the wicked will stumble into ruin.

Proverbs 24:16 HCSB

If you think you can do something, then you can probably do it. If you think you can't do something, then you probably won't do it.

So remember this: if you're having a little trouble getting something done, don't get mad, don't get frustrated, don't get discouraged, and don't give up. Just keep trying . . . and believe in yourself.

When you try hard—and keep trying hard—you can really do amazing things . . . but if you quit at the first sign of trouble, you'll miss out. So here's a good rule to follow: when you have something that you want to finish, finish it . . . and finish it sooner rather than later.

DAY 214
Pray Often

Jesus often slipped away to be alone so he could pray.

Luke 5:16 NCV

Jesus prayed often, and so should you. When you pray, you can tell God the things you need, and you can ask God about the things He wants you to do. The more you pray, the more answers you'll receive from the Father. So, don't wait for bedtime to pray. Make it a habit to pray many times each day.

DAY 215
Pleasing God Is More Important Than Pleasing Friends

For am I now trying to win the favor of people, or God? Or am I striving to please people? If I were still trying to please people, I would not be a slave of Christ.

Galatians 1:10 HCSB

Are you a people-pleaser or a God-pleaser? Hopefully, you're far more concerned with pleasing God than you are with pleasing your friends. But face facts: even if you're a devoted Christian, you're still going to feel the urge to impress your friends—and sometimes that urge will be strong.

Here's your choice: you can choose to please God first, or you can fall victim to peer pressure. The choice is yours—and so are the consequences.

DAY 216
Forgive Other People's Mistakes

I will instruct you and teach you in the way you should go; I will counsel you and watch over you.

Psalm 32:8 NIV

When other people make mistakes, you must find a way to forgive them. And when you make mistakes, as you will from time to time, you must hope that other people will forgive you, too.

When you have done things that you regret, you should apologize, you should clean up the mess you've made, you should learn from your mistakes, and—last but not least—you should forgive yourself. Mistakes happen . . . it's simply a fact of life, and it's simply a part of growing up. So don't be too hard on yourself, especially if you've learned something along the way.

Keep Your Eye Upon the Donut

I can do everything through him that gives me strength.

Philippians 4:13 NIV

Here's a poem that was seen many years ago in a small donut shop:

As you travel through life brother,
Whatever be your goal,
Keep your eye upon the donut,
And not upon the hole.

What do you think these words mean? Well, this little poem can teach you an important lesson: You should spend more time looking at the things you have, not worrying about the things you don't have.

When you think about it, you've got more blessings than you can count. So make it a habit to thank God for the gifts He's given you, and don't feel jealous, angry, or sad about all the other stuff.

Anger Leads to Trouble

Patience is better than strength.

Proverbs 16:32 ICB

In the Book of Proverbs, King Solomon gave us wonderful advice for living wisely. Solomon warned that impatience and anger lead only to trouble. And he was right!

The next time you're tempted to say an unkind word or to throw a temper tantrum, remember Solomon. He was one of the wisest men who ever lived, and he knew that it's always better to be patient. So remain calm and remember that patience is best. After all, if it's good enough for a wise man like Solomon, it should be good enough for us, too.

DAY 219
Beyond Stubbornness

Pride comes before destruction, and an arrogant spirit before a fall.

Proverbs 16:18 HCSB

Since the days of Adam and Eve, human beings have been strong-willed and rebellious. Yet, God's Word warns us to be humble, not prideful. God instructs us to be obedient, not rebellious. God wants us to do things His way. When we do, we earn lots of blessings—more blessings than we can count.

DAY 220
Joyful Abundance

Shout with joy to the LORD, O earth! Worship the LORD with gladness. Come before him, singing with joy.

Psalm 100:1-2 NLT

Have you made the choice to rejoice? Hopefully so. After all, if you're a Christian, you have plenty of reasons to be joyful.

So today, think about this: God has given you too many blessings to count, but you can certainly count some of those blessings. Your job is to honor God with your prayers, your words, your behavior, and your joy.

DAY 221
The Best Time to Praise God

The LORD is my strength and song, and He has become my salvation; He is my God, and I will praise Him.

Exodus 15:2 NIV

When is the best time to praise God? In church? Before dinner is served? At bedtime? None of the above. The best time to praise God is all day, every day, to the greatest extent we can, with thanksgiving in our hearts, and with a song on our lips. Dr. Wayne Oates once admitted, "Many of my prayers are made with my eyes open. You see, it seems I'm always praying about something, and it's not always convenient—or safe—to close my eyes." Dr. Oates understood that God always hears our prayers and that the position of our eyelids is of no concern to Him.

So, find a little more time to lift your concerns to God in prayer, and praise Him for all that He has done. Whether your eyes are open or closed, He's listening.

DAY 222
Honesty Is the Right Policy

Therefore laying aside falsehood, speak truth, each one of you, with his neighbor, for we are members of one another.

Ephesians 4:25 NASB

Sometimes people lie, and sometimes they get away with it. But that doesn't mean that it's wise to lie. And that doesn't make lying the right thing to do. Far from it.

Whatever the problem, lying is always a bad solution. And, besides, lying is always against the will of God. So even if other people lie, don't ever believe that they have lied successfully. There's no such thing as a successful lie.

Making Other People Feel Better

Be gracious in your speech. The goal is to bring out the best in others in a conversation, not put them down, not cut them out.

Colossians 4:6 MSG

Do you like for people to say kind words to you? Of course you do! And that's exactly how other people feel, too. That's why it's so important to say things that make people feel better, not worse.

Your words can help people . . . or not. Make certain that you're the kind of person who says helpful things, not hurtful things. And, make sure that you're the kind of person who helps other people feel better about themselves, not worse.

Be Quick to Forgive

Do to others what you want them to do to you.

Matthew 7:12 NCV

Forgiving other people is hard—sometimes very hard. But God tells us that we must forgive others, even when we'd rather not. So, if you're angry with anybody (or if you're upset by something you yourself have done), it's time to forgive . . . now!

God instructs you to treat other people exactly as you wish to be treated. And since you want to be forgiven for the mistakes that you make, you must be willing to extend forgiveness to other people for the mistakes that they have made. If you can't seem to forgive someone, you should keep asking God to help you until you do. And you can be sure of this: if you keep asking for God's help, He will give it.

DAY 225
God Can Handle It

Now the God of all grace, who called you to His eternal glory in Christ Jesus, will personally restore, establish, strengthen, and support you.

1 Peter 5:10 HCSB

It's a promise that is made over and over again in the Bible: Whatever "it" is, God can handle it.

Life isn't always easy. Far from it! Sometimes, life can be hard, but even then, we're protected by a loving Heavenly Father. When we're worried,

God can help us; when we're sad, God can comfort us. God is not just near, He is here. So we should always lift our thoughts and prayers to Him. When we do, He will answer our prayers. Why? Because He is our shepherd, and He has promised to protect us now and forever.

DAY 226
Happy Thoughts

Those who are pure in their thinking are happy, because they will be with God.

Matthew 5:8 NCV

Do you try to think the kind of thoughts that make you happy, not sad? The Bible says that you should.

Do you try to think about things that are true and right? The Bible says that you should.

Do you turn away from bad thoughts—and away from people who misbehave? The Bible says that you should.

The Bible instructs you to guard your thoughts against things that are hurtful or wrong. So remember this: when you turn away from the bad thoughts and bad people, you've made a very wise choice.

DAY 227
Big Rewards When You Do the Right Thing

Do you want to be counted wise, to build a reputation for wisdom? Here's what you do: Live well, live wisely, live humbly. It's the way you live, not the way you talk, that counts.

James 3:13 MSG

If you open up a dictionary, you'll see that the word "wisdom" means "using good judgement, and knowing what is true." But there's more to it than that. It's not enough to know what's right—if you want to be wise, you must also do what's right.

The Bible promises that when you do smart things, you'll earn big rewards, so slow down and think about things before you do them, not after.

DAY 228
Contentment Now

Keep your lives free from the love of money and be content with what you have, because God has said, "Never will I leave you; never will I forsake you."

Hebrews 13:5 NIV

Where can we find contentment? Is it a result of being wealthy or famous? Nope. Genuine contentment is a gift from God to those who trust Him and follow His commandments.

If we don't find contentment in God, we will never find it anywhere else. But, if we seek Him and obey Him, we will be blessed with joyful, peaceful, meaningful lives. When God dwells at the center of our lives, peace and contentment will belong to us just as surely as we belong to God.

DAY 229
A Helping Hand

Hatred stirs up trouble, but love forgives all wrongs.
Proverbs 10:12 NCV

Sometimes, young people can be very mean. They can make fun of other people, and when they do so, it's wrong. Period.

As Christians, we should be kind to everyone. And, if other kids say unkind things to a child or make fun of him or her, it's up to us to step in, like the Good Samaritan, and lend a helping hand.

So be a girl who is known for your kindness, not for your cruelty. That's how God wants you to behave. Period.

DAY 230
Lies Can Lead to Trouble

Your heart must not be troubled. Believe in God;
believe also in Me.

John 14:1 HCSB

When we tell a lie, trouble starts. Lots of trouble. But when we tell the truth—and nothing but the truth—we stop Old Man Trouble in his tracks.

When we always tell the truth, we make our worries smaller, not bigger. And that's precisely what God wants us to do.

So, if you'd like to have fewer worries and more happiness, abide by this simple rule: tell the truth, the whole truth, and nothing but the truth. When you do, you'll make many of your worries disappear altogether. And that's the truth!

DAY 231
A Forever Love

I am the good shepherd. The good shepherd lays
down his life for the sheep.

John 10:11 NIV

You've probably heard the song "Jesus Loves Me." And exactly how much does He love you? He loves you so much that He gave His life so that you might live forever with Him in heaven.

How can you repay Christ's love? By accepting Him into your heart and by obeying His rules. When you do, He will love you and bless you today, tomorrow, and forever.

Laugh Whenever You Can

A joyful heart is good medicine . . . .

Proverbs 17:22 HCSB

Sometimes, we may feel guilty about having fun when some people around the world are not having any fun at all. But God doesn't want us to spend our lives moping around with frowns on our faces. Far from it! God tells us that a happy heart is a very good thing to have.

So if you're afraid to laugh out loud, don't be. Remember that God wouldn't have given you the gift of laughter if He hadn't intended for you to use it. And remember: if you're laughing, that does not mean that you're unconcerned about people who may be hurting. It simply means that you've taken a little time to have fun, and that's good because God wants you to have a cheerful heart.

DAY 233
Hit a Homerun

Don't be afraid. Only believe.

Mark 5:36 HCSB

His fans called him the "Sultan of Swat." He was Babe Ruth, the baseball player who set records for home runs and strikeouts. Babe's philosophy was simple. He said, "Never let the fear of striking out get in your way." That's smart advice on the diamond or off.

Of course it's never wise to take foolish risks (so buckle up, slow down, and don't do anything stupid!). But when it comes to the game of life, you should not let the fear of failure keep you from taking your swings.

DAY 234
God Loves to Forgive

If we claim that we're free of sin, we're only fooling ourselves. A claim like that is errant nonsense. On the other hand, if we admit our sins—make a clean breast of them—he won't let us down; he'll be true to himself. He'll forgive our sins and purge us of all wrongdoing.

1 John 1:8-9 MSG

Are you perfect? Of course not! Even if you're a very good girl, you're bound to mistakes.

When you make a mistake, you must try your best to learn from it (so that you won't make the very same mistake again). And, if you have hurt someone—or if you have disobeyed God—you must ask for forgiveness. And here's the good news: when you ask for God's forgiveness, He will always give it. God forgives you every single time you ask Him to. So ask!

DAY 235
In His Footsteps

Whoever serves me must follow me. Then my servant will be with me everywhere I am. My Father will honor anyone who serves me.

John 12:26 NCV

Jesus walks with you. Are you walking with Him? Hopefully, you will choose to walk with Him tonight, tomorrow, and every day of your life.

Jesus has called upon believers of every generation (and that includes you) to follow in His footsteps. Will you follow? Please answer that question with a GREAT BIG YES. When you do, your heart will be filled with a GREAT BIG LOVE for Him!

Pray for Everybody

Hatred stirs up trouble, but love forgives all wrongs.

Proverbs 10:12 NCV

It's usually pretty easy to pray for your friends and family members—all you have to do is find the time. But when it comes to praying for people who have hurt you, well that's a different matter entirely!

Like it or not, God says that you've got to pray for the folks you like and for the folks you don't like. Why? Well maybe it's because God knows that He has already forgiven you, and now He thinks it's about time for you to forgive them.

Anger Strikes Out

And be careful that when you get on each other's nerves you don't snap at each other. Look for the best in each other, and always do your best to bring it out.

1 Thessalonians 5:15 MSG

The Bible tells us that we should control our tempers. But sometimes, especially when we're angry or frustrated, our words and our actions may not be so gentle. Sometimes, we may say things or do things that are unkind or hurtful to others. When we do, we're wrong.

The next time you're tempted to strike out in anger, don't. And if you want to help your family and friends, remember that kind words are the kind of words you should speak. Always!

How to Treat Others

See that no one pays back evil for evil, but always try to do good to each other and to everyone else.

I Thessalonians 5:15 TLB

Would you like to make the world a better place? If so, you can start by practicing the Golden Rule.

Jesus said, "Whatever you want others to do for you, do also the same for them" (Matthew 7:12 HCSB). That means that you should treat other people in the very same way that you want to be treated. That's the Golden Rule.

So here's what you should do: if you want to know how to treat somebody, ask the person you see every time you look into the mirror. The answer you receive will tell you exactly what to do.

DAY 239
Always Growing

When I was a child, I spoke like a child, I thought like a child, I reasoned like a child. When I became a man, I put aside childish things.

1 Corinthians 13:11 HCSB

You're growing up day by day, and it's a wonderful thing to watch. Every day, you're learning new things and doing new things. Good for you!

And when should you stop growing up? Hopefully never! That way, you'll always be learning more and doing more.

Do you think it's good to keep growing and growing and growing? If you said "yes," you're right. So remember: you're a very special person today . . . and you'll be just as special when you've grown a little bit more tomorrow.

DAY 240
God's Angels

Don't neglect to show hospitality, for by doing this some have welcomed angels as guests without knowing it.

Hebrews 13:2 HCSB

The Bible has a lot to say about angels. But maybe you've wondered if angels are really real. If so, wonder no more! If the Bible tells you something, you can be sure that it's true.

The Bible teaches us that angels come from God, so that means they are good and they are helpful. We don't need to fear angels, but neither do we need to pretend that they don't exist!

Happiness and Honesty

Lead a quiet and peaceable life in all godliness and honesty.

1 Timothy 2:2 KJV

Have you ever said something that wasn't true? When you did, were you sorry for what you had said? Probably so.

When we're dishonest, we make ourselves unhappy in surprising ways. Here are just a few troubles that result from dishonesty: we feel guilty and we are usually found out and we disappoint others and we disappoint God. It's easy to see that lies always cause more problems than they solve.

Happiness and honesty always go hand in hand. But it's up to you to make sure that you go hand in hand with them!

DAY 242
An Attitude of Kindness

Finally, all of you should be of one mind, full of sympathy toward each other, loving one another with tender hearts and humble minds.

1 Peter 3:8 NLT

An attitude of kindness starts in your heart and works its way out from there.

Do you listen to your heart when it tells you to be kind to other people? Hopefully, you do. After all, lots of people in the world aren't as fortunate as you are—and some of these folks are living very near you.

Ask your parents to help you find ways to do nice things for other people. And don't forget that everybody needs love, kindness, and respect, so you should always be ready to share those things, too.

DAY 243
Listening to Directions

A fool's way is right in his own eyes, but whoever listens to counsel is wise.

Proverbs 12:15 HCSB

Directions, directions, directions. It seems like somebody is always giving you directions: telling you where to go, how to behave, and what to do next. But sometimes all these directions can be confusing! How can you understand everything that everybody tells you? The answer, of course, is that you must pay careful attention to those directions . . . and that means listening.

To become a careful listener, here are some things you must do: 1. Don't talk when you're supposed to be listening (your ears work best when your mouth is closed); 2. Watch the person who's giving the directions (when your eyes and ears work together, it's easier to understand things); 3. If you don't understand something, ask a question (it's better to ask now than to make a mistake later).

Hope Now!

When dreams come true, there is life and joy.

Proverbs 13:12 NLT

Where will you place your hopes today? Will you entrust your future to man or to God? Will you seek solace exclusively from fallible human beings, or will you place your hopes, first and foremost, in the trusting hands of your Creator? The decision is yours, and you must live with the results of the choice you make.

For thoughtful believers, hope begins with God. Period. So today, as you embark upon the next stage of your life's journey, consider the words of the Psalmist: "You are my hope; O Lord GOD, You are my confidence" (71:5 NASB). Then, place your trust in the One who cannot be shaken.

DAY 245
Having Trouble Behaving Yourself? Pray About It!

Rejoice always! Pray constantly. Give thanks in everything, for this is God's will for you in Christ Jesus.

1 Thessalonians 5:16-18 HCSB

Do you really want to become a more obedient girl? Then pray about it. Would you like to learn how to behave yourself a little bit better? Then pray about it. Want to be able to think about things before you get into trouble, not after? Pray for God's help.

If you have questions about whether you should do something or not, pray about it. If there is something you're worried about, ask God to comfort you. And as you pray more, you'll discover that God is always near and that He's always ready to hear from you. So don't worry about things; pray about them. God is waiting to hear from you . . . so what are you waiting for?

Sometimes Sad

Those people who know they have great spiritual needs are happy, because the kingdom of heaven belongs to them. Those who are sad now are happy, because God will comfort them.

Matthew 5:3-4 NCV

Sometimes, you feel happy, and sometimes you don't. When you're feeling sad, here are two very important things you should do: 1. Talk to your parents about your feelings. 2. Talk to God about your feelings.

Talking with your parents is helpful because your mom and dad understand this: The problems that seem VERY BIG to you today probably won't seem so big tomorrow.

Talking with God helps because God hears your prayers and He helps make things better.

So the next time you're sad, don't hold your feelings inside—talk things over with your parents and with God.

DAY 247
Everybody Needs to Hear Kind Words

Avoid irreverent, empty speech, for this will produce an even greater measure of godlessness.

2 Timothy 2:16 HCSB

Your words can help other people . . . or not. So please make sure that you're the kind of girl who says helpful things, not hurtful things. You'll feel better about yourself when you help other people feel better about themselves.

Do you like for people to say kind words to you? Of course you do! And that's exactly how other people feel, too. That's why it's so important to say things that make people feel better, not worse.

Everybody needs to hear kind words, and that's exactly the kind of words they should hear from you!

DAY 248
Thanking Those Who Serve

There are different kinds of gifts, but they are all from the same Spirit. There are different ways to serve but the same Lord to serve.

1 Corinthians 12:4–5 NCV

Jesus instructed His disciples to help each other. Those instructions still apply. If we are to be obedient servants of Christ, we must be willing to help those who can't help themselves. In other words, we must become "servants to all."

Some people choose careers that allow them to serve and protect our homes and our world (this includes police officers, firefighters, and those who serve in our military). These brave men and women make very big sacrifices, and we should thank them whenever we can.

So let's all offer prayers of thanks for those brave men and women who serve and protect us . . . and let's all do our best to serve other people wherever we can.

DAY 249
Putting Things Off Until the Last Minute

Therefore, get your minds ready for action, being self-disciplined, and set your hope completely on the grace to be brought to you at the revelation of Jesus Christ.

1 Peter 1:13 HCSB

When you know that something really needs to be done, you have a choice to make: you can either do the work that needs to be done, or you can put it off till later. If you get into the habit of doing things in a timely manner, you'll feel better about yourself, and you'll earn bigger rewards from life.

So, when you know that it's time to do something, just go ahead and do it. It's the smart thing to do and the best way to live.

DAY 250
Questions?

An indecisive man is unstable in all his ways.

James 1:8 HCSB

God doesn't explain Himself in ways that we humans would prefer (think about this: if God did explain Himself perfectly, we wouldn't have enough brainpower to understand the explanation that He gave!).

When innocent people are hurt, we question God because we can't figure out exactly what He's doing, or why. But even when we can't answer tough questions like these, we must trust in God's love, God's wisdom, and God's plan.

And while we're waiting for that wonderful day when all our questions will be answered (in heaven), we should use the time that we have here on earth to help the people who need it most.

DAY 251
A Cheerful Heart

Jacob said, "For what a relief it is to see your friendly smile. It is like seeing the smile of God!"

Genesis 33:10 NLT

The Bible tells us that a cheerful heart is like medicine: it makes us feel better. Where does cheerfulness begin? It begins inside each of us; it begins in the heart. So let's be thankful to God for His blessings, and let's show our thanks by sharing good cheer wherever we go.

Today, make sure that you share a smile and a kind word with as many people as you can. This old world needs all the cheering up it can get . . . and so do your friends.

DAY 252
A God of Possibilities

But Jesus looked at them and said, "With men this is impossible, but with God all things are possible."

Matthew 19:26 HCSB

If you really want to know God, you must be willing to worship Him seven days a week, not just on Sunday.

Every life, including yours, is based upon some form of worship. The question is not whether you will worship, but what you worship. If you choose to worship God, you will receive a king-sized harvest of blessings. So, worship Him with sincerity and thanksgiving. Write His name on your heart and rest assured that He, too, has written your name on His.

DAY 253
Think Good Thoughts

Come near to God, and God will come near to you. You sinners, clean sin out of your lives. You who are trying to follow God and the world at the same time, make your thinking pure.

James 4:8 NCV

Do you try to think good thoughts about your friends, your family, and yourself? The Bible says that you should. Do you lift your hopes and your prayers to God many times each day? The Bible says that you should. Do you say "no" to people who want you to do bad things or think bad thoughts? The Bible says that you should.

The Bible teaches you to guard your thoughts against things that are hurtful or wrong. So remember this: When you turn away from bad thoughts and turn instead toward God and His Son Jesus, you will be protected . . . and you will be blessed.

DAY 254
Getting to Know God

Stay clear of silly stories that get dressed up as religion. Exercise daily in God—no spiritual flabbiness, please!

I Timothy 4:7 MSG

Want to know God better? Then schedule a meeting with Him every day.

Each day has 1,440 minutes—will you spend a few of those minutes with your Heavenly Father? He deserves that much of your time and more. God wants you to pay attention to Him. So, if you haven't already done so, form the habit of spending quality time with your Creator. He deserves it . . . and so, for that matter, do you.

DAY 255
Tell It Like It Is

I have no greater joy than this: to hear that my children are walking in the truth.

3 John 1:4 HCSB

Perhaps you've heard the story of the boy who cried "wolf!" In that story, the boy exaggerated his problems and eventually got himself into BIG trouble!

When we pretend that our troubles are worse than they really are, we may earn a little sympathy now, but we'll invite lots of trouble later.

If you're ever tempted to cry wolf, don't. Exaggeration wasn't good for the boy who cried wolf, and it's not good for you.

DAY 256
Self-defeating Anger

When you are angry, do not sin, and be sure to stop being angry before the end of the day. Do not give the devil a way to defeat you.

Ephesians 4:26–27 NCV

When you allow yourself to become angry, you are certain to defeat at least one person: yourself. When you allow the minor frustrations of everyday life to hijack your emotions, you do harm to yourself and to your loved ones. So today and every day, guard yourself against the kind of angry thinking that inevitably takes a toll on your emotions and your relationships.

DAY 257
Do Yourself a Favor

And whenever you stand praying, if you have anything against anyone, forgive him, so that your Father in heaven may also forgive you your wrongdoing.

Mark 11:25 HCSB

When you forgive somebody else, you're actually doing yourself a favor. Why? Because when you forgive the other person, you get rid of angry feelings that can make you unhappy.

Are you still angry about something that happened yesterday, or the day before that, or the day before that? Do yourself a big favor: forgive everybody (including yourself, if necessary). When you do, you won't change what happened yesterday, but you will make today a whole lot better.

DAY 258
Encourage Each Other

So encourage each other and give each other strength, just as you are doing now.

1 Thessalonians 5:11 NCV

When other people are sad, what can we do? We can do our best to cheer them up by showing kindness and love.

The Bible tells us that we must care for each other, and when everybody is happy, that's an easy thing to do. But, when people are sad, for whatever reason, it's up to us to speak a kind word or to offer a helping hand.

Do you know someone who is discouraged or sad? If so, perhaps it's time to take matters into your own hands. Think of something you can do to cheer that person up . . . and then do it! You'll make two people happy.

Love That Lasts

It is good and pleasant when God's people live together in peace!

Psalm 133:1 NCV

Are your friends kind to you? And are your friends nice to other people, too? If so, congratulations! If not, it's probably time to start looking for a few new friends. After all, it's really not very much fun to be around people who aren't nice to everybody.

The Bible teaches that a pure heart is a wonderful blessing. It's up to each of us to fill our hearts with love for God, love for Jesus, and love for all people. When we do, we feel better about ourselves.

Do you want to be the best person you can be? Then invite the love of Christ into your heart and share His love with your family and friends. And remember that lasting love always comes from a pure heart . . . like yours!

DAY 260
Gentle Words

Always be humble, gentle, and patient, accepting each other in love.

Ephesians 4:2 NCV

The Bible tells us that gentle words are helpful and that cruel words are not. But sometimes, especially when we're upset, our words and our actions may not be so gentle. Sometimes, we may say things that are unkind or hurtful to others. But it's wrong to hurt others.

So the next time you're tempted to say something or do something in a fit of anger, don't. And while you're at it, remember that gentle words are better than angry words and good deeds are better than the other kind. Always!

DAY 261
God's Promise of Love

His banner over me was love.

Song of Solomon 2:4 KJV

In the Bible, God makes this amazing promise—He promises that He loves you. And it's a promise that He intends to keep.

No matter where you are (and no matter what you've done), you're never beyond the reach of God's love. So take time tonight (and every night) to thank Him for love that is too big to understand with your head, but not too big to feel with your heart.

DAY 262
The Futility of Foolish Arguments

But stay away from those who have foolish arguments and talk about useless family histories and argue and quarrel about the law. Those things are worth nothing and will not help anyone.

Titus 3:9 NCV

Time and again, God's Word warns us that most arguments are a monumental waste of time, of energy, of life. In Titus, we are warned to refrain from "foolish arguments," and with good reason. Such arguments usually do more for the devil than they do for God.

So the next time you're tempted to engage in a silly squabble, stop yourself before you lose your temper. When you do, you'll put a smile on God's face, and you'll send the devil packing.

DAY 263
It Helps to Be Patient

Patience is better than pride.

Ecclesiastes 7:8 NLT

Most of us are impatient for God to grant us the desires of our heart. Usually, we know what we want, and we know precisely when we want it: right now, if not sooner. But God may have other plans. And when God's plans differ from our own, we must trust in His infinite wisdom and in His infinite love.

God instructs us to be patient in all things. We must be patient with our families, with our friends, and with our acquaintances. We must also be patient with our Heavenly Father as He unfolds His plan for our lives. And that's as it should be. After all, think how patient God has been with us.

Self-Control and Patience

All athletes practice strict self-control. They do it to win a prize that will fade away, but we do it for an eternal prize.

1 Corinthians 9:25 NLT

The Book of Proverbs tells us that self-control and patience are very good things to have. But for most of us, self-control and patience can also be very hard things to learn.

Are you having trouble being patient? And are you having trouble slowing down long enough to think before you act? If so, remember that self-control takes practice, and lots of it, so keep trying. And if you make a mistake, don't be too upset. After all, if you're going to be a really patient person, you shouldn't just be patient with others; you should also be patient with yourself.

If You Don't Know What to Say

Watch the way you talk. Let nothing foul or dirty come out of your mouth. Say only what helps, each word a gift.

Ephesians 4:29 MSG

Sometimes, it's hard to know exactly what to say. And sometimes, it can be very tempting to say something that isn't true—or something that isn't nice. But when you say things you shouldn't say, you'll regret it later.

So make this promise to yourself, and keep it—promise to think about the things you say before you say them. And whatever you do, always tell the truth. When you do these things, you'll be doing yourself a big favor, and you'll be obeying the Word of God.

DAY 266
Letting Other People Know What It Means to Be a Christian

But respect Christ as the holy Lord in your hearts. Always be ready to answer everyone who asks you to explain about the hope you have.

1 Peter 3:15 NCV

Every Christian, each in his or her own way, has a responsibility to share the Good News of our Jesus. And it's important to remember that we bear testimony through both words and actions. Wise Christians follow the advice of St. Francis of Assisi who advised, "Preach the gospel at all times and, if necessary, use words."

As you think about how your example influences others, remember that actions speak louder than words . . . much louder!

DAY 267
When We're Worried

Give all your worries and cares to God, for he cares about what happens to you.

1 Peter 5:6 NLT

When we're worried, there are two places we should take our concerns: to the people who love and care for us and to God.

When troubles arise, it helps to talk about them with parents, grandparents, and concerned adults. But we shouldn't stop there: we should also talk to God through our prayers.

If you're worried about something, you can pray about it any time you want. And remember that God is always listening, and He always wants to hear from you.

So when you're worried, try this plan: talk and pray. Talk to the grown-ups who love you, and pray to the Heavenly Father who made you. The more you talk and the more you pray, the better you'll feel.

DAY 268
Don't Whine!

Words kill, words give life; they're either poison or fruit—you choose.

Proverbs 18:21 MSG

Do you like to listen to other children whine? No way! And since you don't like to hear other kids whining, then you certainly shouldn't whine, either.

Sometimes, kids think that whining is a good way to get the things they want . . . but it's not! So if your parents or your teacher ask you to do something, don't complain about it. And if there's something you want, don't whine and complain until you get it.

Remember: whining won't make you happy . . . and it won't make anybody else happy, either.

DAY 269
The Truth

Go after a life of love as if your life depended on it—because it does. Give yourselves to the gifts God gives you. Most of all, try to proclaim his truth.

1 Corinthians 14:1 MSG

Jesus had a message for His followers. He said, "The truth will set you free." When we do the right thing and tell the truth, we don't need to worry about our lies catching up with us. When we behave honestly, we don't have to worry about feeling guilty or ashamed. But, if we fail to do what we know is right, bad things start to happen, and we feel guilty.

Jesus understood that the truth is a very good thing indeed. We should understand it, too. And we should keep telling it as long as we live.

DAY 270
Because You're a Christian

Make the Master proud of you by being good citizens. Respect the authorities, whatever their level; they are God's emissaries for keeping order.

1 Peter 2:13-14 MSG

Do you behave differently because you're a Christian? Or do you behave in pretty much the same way that you would if you had never heard of Jesus? Hopefully, your behavior is better because of the things you've learned from the Bible.

Doing the right thing is not always easy, especially when you're tired or frustrated. But, doing the wrong thing almost always leads to trouble. So here's some advice: remember the lessons you learn from the Bible. And keep remembering them every day of your life.

Every Day Is a Special Day

David and the whole house of Israel were celebrating before the Lord.

2 Samuel 6:5 HCSB

Every day should be a time for celebration, and hopefully, you feel like celebrating! After all, this day (like every other day) gives you the chance to thank God for all the wonderful things He has given you.

So don't wait for birthdays or holidays—make every day a special day, including this one. Take time to pause and thank God for His gifts. He deserves your thanks, and you deserve to celebrate!

That Little Voice

For God is pleased with you when, for the sake of your conscience, you patiently endure unfair treatment.

1 Peter 2:19 NLT

When you know that you're doing what's right, you'll feel better about yourself. Why? Because you have a little voice in your head called your "conscience." Your conscience is a feeling that tells you whether something is right or wrong—and it's a feeling that makes you feel better about yourself when you know you've done the right thing.

Your conscience is an important tool. Pay attention to it!

The more you listen to your conscience, the easier it is to behave yourself. So here's great advice: first, slow down long enough to figure out the right thing to do—and then do it! When you do, you'll be proud of yourself . . . and other people will be proud of you, too.

DAY 273
When Things Go Wrong

But as for you, be strong; don't be discouraged, for your work has a reward.

2 Chronicles 15:7 HCSB

Face facts: some days are more wonderful than other days. Sometimes, everything seems to go right, and on other days, many things seem to go wrong. But here's something to remember: even when you're disappointed with the way things turn out, God is near . . . and He loves you very much!

If you're disappointed, worried, sad, or afraid, you can talk to your parents and to God. And you certainly feel better when you do!

DAY 274
What a Friend!

Just as the Father has loved Me, I have also loved you; abide in My love.

John 15:9 NASB

Do you know that Jesus loves you? And have you thought about exactly what His love should mean to you? Well, Christ's love should make you feel better about your life, your family, your future, and yourself.

There's an old song that says, "What a friend we have in Jesus." Those words are certainly true! When you invite Him into your heart, Jesus will be your friend forever.

Jesus wants you to have a happy, healthy life. He wants you to behave yourself, and He wants you to feel good about yourself. And now, it's up to you to do your best to live up to the hopes and dreams of your very best friend: Jesus.

Wisdom

Do not deceive yourselves. If any one of you thinks he is wise by the standards of this age, he should become a "fool" so that he may become wise. For the wisdom of this world is foolishness in God's sight.

I Corinthians 3:18-19 NIV

If you look in a dictionary, you'll see that the word "wisdom" means "using good judgement, and knowing what is true." But there's more: it's not just enough to know what's right; if you really want to become a wise person, you must also do what's right.

A big part of "doing what's right" is learning self-control . . . and the best day to start learning self-control is this one!

How Would Jesus Behave?

You did not choose Me, but I chose you. I appointed you that you should go out and produce fruit, and that your fruit should remain, so that whatever you ask the Father in My name, He will give you.

John 15:16 HCSB

If you're not certain whether something is right or wrong, ask yourself a simple question: "What would Jesus do if He were here?" The answer to that question will tell you how to behave yourself.

Jesus was perfect, but we are not. Still, we must try as hard as we can to be like Him. When we do, we will love others, just like Christ loves all of us.

DAY 277
His Promises Never Fail

Patient endurance is what you need now, so you will continue to do God's will. Then you will receive all that he has promised.

Hebrews 10:36 NLT

God has made plenty of promises to you, and He will most certainly keep them all. You can find these promises in the book God wrote. It's called the Bible, and you probably already own at least one or two copies.

The Bible is your guide for life here on earth and for life eternal—as a believer, you are called upon to trust its promises, to follow its commandments, and to share its Good News—beginning now and ending never.

God Knows Best

However, each one must live his life in the situation the Lord assigned when God called him.

1 Corinthians 7:17 HCSB

Here are three things to think about: 1. God loves you. 2. God wants what's best for you. 3. God has a plan for you.

God's plan may not always happen exactly like you want, but remember: God always knows best. Sometimes, even though you may want something very badly, you must still be patient and wait for the right time to get it, And the right time, of course, is determined by God.

Even if you don't get exactly what you want today, you can be sure that God wants what's best for you . . . today, tomorrow, and forever.

Behaving Yourself

So don't get tired of doing what is good. Don't get discouraged and give up, for we will reap a harvest of blessing at the appropriate time.

Galatians 6:9 NLT

Doing the right thing isn't always easy, especially when we're tired or frustrated. But, doing the wrong thing almost always leads to trouble. And sometimes, it leads to BIG trouble.

When you do the right thing, you don't have to worry about what you did or what you said. But, if you are dishonest—or if you do something that you know is wrong—you'll be worried that someone will find out. So do the right thing; it may be harder in the beginning, but it's easier in the end.

DAY 280
Learning to Share

Be generous: Invest in acts of charity. Charity yields high returns.

Ecclesiastes 11:1 MSG

Lots of people in the world aren't as fortunate as you are. Some of these folks live in faraway places, and that makes it harder to help them. But other people who need your help are living near you.

Ask your parents to help you find ways to do something nice for folks who need it. And don't forget that everybody needs love, kindness, and respect, so you should always be ready to share those things, too.

DAY 281
Where Does God Fit In?

Every morning he wakes me. He teaches me to listen like a student. The Lord God helps me learn...

Isaiah 50:4-5 NCV

Where does God fit in to your life? Do you "squeeze Him in" on Sundays and at mealtimes? Or do you talk to Him more often than that?

Even if you're the busiest kid on the planet, you can still make time for God. When you think about it, isn't that the very least you should do?

DAY 282
Words Worthy of Our Savior

When you talk, do not say harmful things, but say what people need—words that will help others become stronger. Then what you say will do good to those who listen to you.

Ephesians 4:29 NCV

Are you a person who consistently uses words that are pleasing to God? Hopefully so. If you genuinely desire to be a good person, your words and your actions must demonstrate your faithfulness to the Creator.

Of course you must never take the Lord's name in vain, but it doesn't stop there. You must also try to speak words of encouragement, words that lift others up, words that give honor to your Heavenly Father.

The Bible clearly warns that you will be judged by the words you speak, so choose those words carefully. Remember this: God is always listening.

The Power of Kindness

If you really carry out the royal law prescribed in Scripture, You shall love your neighbor as yourself, you are doing well.

James 2:8 HCSB

Just as Christ has been—and will always be— the ultimate friend to His flock, so should we be Christlike in the kindness and generosity that we show toward others, especially those who are most in need.

When we walk each day with Jesus—and obey the commandments found in God's Holy Word— we become worthy ambassadors for Christ. When we share the love of Christ, we share a priceless gift with the world.

The Powerful Life

God's Way is not a matter of mere talk; it's an empowered life.

I Corinthians 4:20 MSG

How do people know that you're a Christian? Well, you can tell them, of course. And make no mistake about it: talking about your faith in God is a very good thing to do. But telling people about Jesus isn't enough. You should also show people how a Christian (like you) should behave.

God wants you to be loving and giving. That way, when another person sees how you behave, that person will know what it means to be a good Christian . . . a good Christian like you!

Stop Fighting

It's a mark of good character to avert quarrels, but fools love to pick fights.

Proverbs 20:3 MSG

Since the days of Cain and Abel, people have discovered plenty of things to fight about (Cain and Abel, by the way, were the sons of Adam and

Eve). It seems that fighting is a favorite activity for many people, even though it's almost always the wrong thing to do.

Kids should do their best to avoid fights, period. So do yourself a favor: try to avoid senseless scuffles, foolish fights, alarming arguments, and constant conflicts. You'll be glad you did . . . and so will God.

DAY 286
The Joyful Life

Always be full of joy in the Lord. I say it again— rejoice!

Philippians 4:4 NLT

A man named C. S. Lewis once said, "Joy is the serious business of heaven." And he was right! God seriously wants you to be a seriously joyful person.

One way that you can have a more joyful life is by learning how to become a more obedient person. When you do, you'll stay out of trouble, and you'll have lots more time for fun.

So here's a way to be a more joyful, happy person: do the right thing! It's the best way to live.

Don't Grow Tired of Forgiving

Then Peter came to him and asked, "Lord, how often should I forgive someone who sins against me? Seven times?" "No!" Jesus replied, "seventy times seven!"

Matthew 18:21-22 NLT

How often does God forgive us? More times than we can count! And that, by the way, is exactly how many times that God expects us to forgive other people—more times than we care to count.

Of this you can be sure: God won't ever get tired of forgiving you. And, because He has forgiven you, He doesn't want you to get tired of forgiving other people . . . ever!

Pay Attention to Your Bible

All Scripture is inspired by God and is profitable for teaching, for rebuking, for correcting, for training in righteousness, so that the man of God may be complete, equipped for every good work.

2 Timothy 3:16-17 HCSB

Do you think about the Bible a lot . . . or not? Hopefully, you pay careful attention to the things you learn from God's Word! After all, the Bible is God's message to you. It's not just a book, it's a priceless, one-of-a-kind treasure . . . and it has amazing things to teach you. So start learning about the Bible now, and keep learning about it for as long as you live!

Obeying God and Being Happy

I will praise you, Lord, with all my heart. I will tell all the miracles you have done. I will be happy because of you; God Most High, I will sing praises to your name.

Psalm 9:1-2 NCV

Do you want to be happy? Here are some things you should do: Love God and His Son, Jesus; obey the Golden Rule; and always try to do the right thing. When you do these things, you'll discover that happiness goes hand-in-hand with good behavior.

The happiest people do not misbehave; they are not cruel or greedy. The happiest people don't say unkind things. The happiest people are those who love God and follow His rules—starting, of course, with the Golden one.

DAY 290
Promises You Can Trust

Do not be afraid or discouraged. For the LORD your God is with you wherever you go.

Joshua 1:9 NLT

God has made quite a few promises to you, and He intends to keep every single one of them. You will find these promises in a book like no other: the Holy Bible. The Bible is your map for life here on earth and for life in heaven.

God's promises never fail and they never grow old. You must trust those promises and share them with your family, with your friends, and with the world . . . starting now . . . and ending never.

DAY 291
Developing New Habits

For every tree is known by its own fruit.

Luke 6:44 NKJV

Perhaps you've tried to become a more patient person, but you're still falling back into your old habits. If so, don't get discouraged. Instead, become even more determined to become the person God wants you to be.

If you trust God, and if you keep asking Him to help you change bad habits, He will help you make yourself into a new person. So, if at first you don't succeed, keep praying. If you keep asking, you'll eventually get the answers you need.

DAY 292
Real Love

For the LORD your God has arrived to live among you. He is a mighty savior. He will rejoice over you with great gladness. With his love, he will calm all your fears. He will exult over you by singing a happy song.

Zephaniah 3:17 NLT

How big is God's love for you? As long as you're alive, you'll never be able to figure it out because God's love is just too big to understand. But this much we know: God loves you so much that He sent His Son Jesus to come to this earth so you could live forever in heaven.

God's love is bigger and more powerful than anybody can imagine, but His love is very real. So do yourself a favor right now: accept God's love with open arms and welcome His Son Jesus into your heart. When you do, your life will be changed today, tomorrow, and forever.

DAY 293
God Knows My Heart

Create in me a pure heart, God, and make my spirit right again.

Psalm 51:10 NCV

Other people see you from the outside. God sees you from the inside—God sees your heart.

Kindness comes from the heart. So does sharing. So if you want to show your family and your friends that your heart is filled with kindness and love, one way to do it is by sharing. But don't worry about trying to show God what kind of person you are. He already knows your heart, and He loves you more than you can imagine.

DAY 294
Honesty Begins at Home

Good people will be guided by honesty.

Proverbs 11:3 ICB

Should you be honest with your parents? Certainly. With your brothers and sisters? Of course. With cousins, grandparents, aunts, and uncles? Yes! In fact, you should be honest with everybody in your family because honesty starts at home.

If you can't be honest in your own house, how can you expect to be honest in other places, like at church or at school? So make sure that you're completely honest with your family. If you are, then you're much more likely to be honest with everybody else.

Sharing Love and Kindness

Talk and act like a person expecting to be judged by the Rule that sets us free. For if you refuse to act kindly, you can hardly expect to be treated kindly. Kind mercy wins over harsh judgment every time.

James 2:12-13 MSG

Where does kindness start? It starts in our hearts and works its way out from there. Jesus taught us that a pure heart is a wonderful blessing. It's up to each of us to fill our hearts with love for God, love for Jesus, and love for all people. When we do, we are blessed.

Do you want to be the best person you can be? Then invite the love of Christ into your heart and share His love with your family and friends. And remember that lasting love always comes from a pure heart . . . like yours!

Doing the Right Thing

Do what is right and good in the Lord's sight, so that you may prosper and so that you may enter and possess the good land the Lord your God swore to [give] your fathers.

Deuteronomy 6:18 HCSB

Oswald Chambers advised, "Never support an experience which does not have God as its source, and faith in God as its result." These words serve as a powerful reminder that, as Christians, we are called to walk with God and obey His commandments. But, we live in a world that presents us with countless temptations to stray far from God's path. We Christians, when confronted with sin, have clear instructions: Walk—or better yet run—in the opposite direction.

Living by God's Rules

Does the LORD delight in burnt offerings and sacrifices as much as in obeying the voice of the LORD? To obey is better than sacrifice . . . .

1 Samuel 15:22 NIV

God has rules, and He wants you to obey them. He wants you to be fair, honest, and kind. He wants you to behave yourself, and He wants you to respect your parents. God has other rules, too, and you'll find them in a very special book: the Bible.

With a little help from your parents, you can figure out God's rules. And then, it's up to you to live by them. When you do, everybody will be pleased—you'll be pleased, your parents will be pleased . . . and God will be pleased, too.

When Bad Things Happen

I leave you peace; my peace I give you. I do not give it to you as the world does. So don't let your hearts be troubled or afraid.

John 14:27 NCV

When bad things happen, it's understandable that we might feel afraid. In fact, it's good to be afraid if our fears keep us from behaving foolishly (by the way, if that little voice inside your head tells you that doing something is dangerous, don't do it).

When our own troubles—or the world's troubles—leave us fearful, we should discuss our concerns with the people who love and care for us.

Parents and grandparents can help us understand our fears, and they can help us feel better. That's why we need to talk with them.

It's okay to be afraid—all of us are fearful from time to time. And it's good to know that we can talk about our fears with loved ones and with God. When we do, we'll discover that fear lasts for a little while, but love lasts forever.

DAY 299
Follow Jesus

"Follow Me," Jesus told them, "and I will make you into fishers of men!" Immediately they left their nets and followed Him.

Mark 1:17-18 HCSB

Tomorrow morning when you wake up, who will you walk with? Do yourself a favor—walk with Jesus!

God's Word promises that when you follow in Christ's footsteps, you will learn how to behave yourself, and you'll learn how to live a good life. Jesus wants you to be a "new creation" through Him. And that's exactly what you should want for yourself, too. So talk with Jesus (through prayer) and walk with Him (by obeying His rules) today and forever.

DAY 300
Expecting God's Blessings

My cup runs over. Surely goodness and mercy shall follow me all the days of my life; and I will dwell in the house of the Lord forever.

Face facts: Christians have every reason to be optimistic and hopeful about life here on earth and life eternal. Mrs. Charles E. Cowman advised, "Never yield to gloomy anticipation. Place your hope and confidence in God. He has no record of failure."

So, be a hope-filled Christian. Think optimistically about your life, your family, and your future. It's the right way to think and the right way to live.

DAY 301
A Great Big Thank You

Praise the LORD. Give thanks to the LORD, for he is good; his love endures forever.

Psalm 106:1 NIV

If you're like most girls you're very busy doing things and learning things. But no matter how

211

busy you are—even if you hardly have a moment to spare—you should still slow down and say "Thank You," to God!

God has given you many things, and you owe Him everything, including a GREAT BIG THANK YOU, starting now (and ending never!).

Who Rules?

Do not worship any other gods besides me.

Exodus 20:3 NLT

Who rules your heart? Is it God, or is it something else?

In the book of Exodus, God warns that we should place no gods before Him. Yet all too often, we place our Lord in second, third, or fourth place as we worship the gods of pride, greed, power, or personal gratification. When we unwittingly place possessions or relationships above our love for the Creator, we must seek His forgiveness and change our ways.

Does God rule your heart? Make certain that the honest answer to this question is a resounding yes. In the life of every righteous believer, God comes first. And that's precisely the place that He deserves in your heart.

DAY 303
Parents Know Best!

Success, success to you, and success to those who help you, for your God will help you....

1 Chronicles 12:18 NIV

God makes this promise: If you have faith in Him, you can do BIG things! So if you have something important to do, pray about it and ask God for help. When you ask God to help you, He will. And while you're at it, never be afraid to ask your parents for help.

When you talk things over with your parents, you'll soon discover that they want you to do BIG things . . . and they can give you LOTS of help.

DAY 304
Think About What's Right

Keep your eyes focused on what is right. Keep looking straight ahead to what is good.

Proverbs 4:25 ICB

In the Book of Proverbs, King Solomon gave us wonderful advice for living wisely. Solomon said that we should keep our eyes "focused on what is right." In other words, we should do our best to say and do the things that we know are pleasing to God.

If you're tempted to say an unkind word or to say something that isn't true, remember the advice of King Solomon. He knew that it's always better to do the right thing, even when it's tempting to do otherwise. So if you know something is wrong, don't do it; instead, do what you know to be right. When you do, you'll be saving yourself a lot of trouble and you'll be obeying the Word of God.

DAY 305
You Feel Better About Yourself When You Share

Be generous to the poor—you'll never go hungry; shut your eyes to their needs, and run a gauntlet of curses.

Proverbs 28:27 MSG

The more you share, the quicker you'll discover this fact: Good things happen to people (like you) who are kind enough to share the blessings that God has given them.

Sharing makes you feel better about yourself. Whether you're at home or at school, remember that the best rewards go to the kids who are kind and generous—not to the people who are unkind or stingy. So do what's right: share. You'll feel lots better about yourself when you do.

Trusting God

"I say this because I know what I am planning for you," says the Lord. "I have good plans for you, not plans to hurt you. I will give you hope and a good future."

Jeremiah 29:11 NCV

Sometimes, things happen that we simply don't understand. That's exactly how God intends it! You see God has given us many gifts, but He hasn't given us the power to understand everything that happens in our world (that comes later, when we get to heaven!).

The Bible tells us God's plans are far bigger than we can possibly understand. That's one of the reasons that God doesn't make His plans clear to us. But even when we can't understand why God allows certain things to happen, we can trust His love for us.

The Bible does make one part of God's plan perfectly clear: we should accept His Son Jesus into our hearts so that we might have eternal life (John 3:16). When we do, we are protected forever.

The Kid in the Mirror

For you made us only a little lower than God, and you crowned us with glory and honor.

Psalm 8:5 NLT

Do you really like the person you see when you look into the mirror? You should! After all, the person in the mirror is a very special person who is made—and loved—by God.

In fact, you are loved in many, many ways: God loves you, your parents love you, and your family loves you, for starters. So you should love yourself, too.

So here's something to think about: since God thinks you're special, and since so many people think you're special, isn't it about time for you to agree with them? Of course it is! It's time to say, "You're very wonderful and very special," to the person you see in the mirror.

The Joy of Serving God

Enjoy serving the Lord, and he will give you what you want.

Psalm 37:4 NCV

Are you excited about serving God? You should be. As a believer living in today's challenging world, you have countless opportunities to honor your Father in heaven by serving Him.

Far too many Christians seem bored with their faith and stressed by their service. Don't allow yourself to become one of them! Serve God with thanksgiving in your heart and praise on your lips. Make your service to Him a time of celebration and thanksgiving. Worship your Creator by working for Him, joyfully, faithfully, and often.

DAY 309
Honesty Pays

Therefore, whatever you want others to do for you, do also the same for them—this is the Law and the Prophets.

Matthew 7:12 HCSB

Do you want other people to be honest with you? Of course you do. And that's why you should be honest with them. The words of Matthew 7:12 remind us that, as believers in Christ, we should treat others as we wish to be treated. And that means telling them the truth!

The Golden Rule is your tool for deciding how you will treat other people. When you use the

Golden Rule as your guide for living, your words and your actions will be pleasing to other people and to God.

DAY 310
God's Greatest Promise

I assure you: Anyone who believes has eternal life.

It's time to remind yourself of a promise that God made a long time ago—the promise that God sent His Son Jesus to save the world and to save you! And when you stop to think about it, there can be no greater promise than that.

No matter where you are, God is with you. God loves you, and He sent His Son so that you can live forever in heaven with your loved ones. WOW! That's the greatest promise in the history of the universe. The End.

DAY 311
Asking God

Until now you have not asked for anything in my name. Ask and you will receive, so that your joy will be the fullest possible joy.

John 16:24 NCV

What should you do if you need something? Well, of course you can ask your parents, but you shouldn't stop there. You can also ask for God's help, too.

The Bible makes it clear that when you need help, you can always ask God. You shouldn't just ask Him one time. You should keep asking for His help. While you're at it, you should do your fair share of the work, trusting that when you've done your best, it's up to God to do the rest.

DAY 312
It's Not Hard to Be Kind

Therefore, God's chosen ones, holy and loved, put on heartfelt compassion, kindness, humility, gentleness, and patience.

Colossians 3:12 HCSB

How hard is it to say a kind word? Not very! Yet sometimes we're so busy that we forget to say the very things that might make other people feel better.

We should always try to say nice things to our families and friends. And when we feel like saying something that's not so nice, perhaps we should stop and think before we say it. Kind words help; cruel words hurt. It's as simple as that. And, when we say the right thing at the right time, we give a gift that can change someone's day or someone's life.

Listen to Your Parents

Listen carefully to wisdom; set your mind on understanding.

Proverbs 2:2 NCV

Are you the kind of girl who listens carefully to the things your parents tell you? You should. Your parents want the very best for you. They want you to be happy and healthy; they want you to be smart and to do smart things. Your parents have much to teach you, and you have much to learn. So listen carefully to the things your mom and dad have to say. And ask lots of questions. When you do, you'll soon discover that your parents have lots of answers . . . lots of very good answers.

God Teaches Us

If you hide your sins, you will not succeed. If you confess and reject them, you will receive mercy.

Proverbs 28:13 NCV

The Bible says that when people make mistakes, God corrects them. And that means that if you make a mistake, God will try to find a way to teach you how to keep from making that same mistake again.

God doesn't expect you to be perfect, but He does expect you to learn from your mistakes— NOW!

When Friends Misbehave

Whoever walks with the wise will become wise; whoever walks with fools will suffer harm.

Proverbs 13:20 NLT

If you're like most people, you have probably been tempted to "go along with the crowd" . . . even when the crowd was misbehaving. But here's something to think about: just because your friends may be misbehaving doesn't mean that you have to misbehave, too.

When people behave badly, they can spoil things in a hurry. So make sure that they don't spoil things for you.

So, if your friends misbehave, don't copy them! Instead, do the right thing. You'll be glad you did . . . and so will God!

DAY 316
The Best Time to Be Obedient

The one who has My commandments and keeps them is the one who loves Me. And the one who loves Me will be loved by My Father. I also will love him and will reveal Myself to him.

John 14:21 HCSB

When is the best time to be obedient? It's always the right time to obey your parents, your teachers, and your Father in heaven.

It's not enough to know what's right; if you really want to become a better person, you must also do what's right. Starting now, and stopping never.

DAY 317
Your Prayers

When a believing person prays, great things happen.

James 5:16 NCV

Okay, from the looks of things, you're an extremely busy girl. And perhaps, because of your demanding schedule, you've neglected to pay sufficient attention to a particularly important part of your life: the spiritual part. If so, today is the day to change, and one way to make that change is simply to spend a little more time talking with God.

God is trying to get His message through to you. Are you listening? If so, congratulations. If not, try praying a little more each day.

DAY 318
Patience and the Golden Rule

Always be humble and gentle. Be patient and accept each other with love.

Ephesians 4:2 ICB

Jesus gave us a Golden Rule for living: He said that we should treat other people in the same way that we want to be treated. And because we want other people to be patient with us, we, in turn, must be patient with them.

Being patient with other people means treating them with kindness, respect, and understanding. It means waiting our turn when we're standing in line and forgiving our friends when they've done something we don't like. Sometimes, it's hard to be patient, but we've got to do our best. And when we do, we're following the Golden Rule—God's rule for how to treat others—and everybody wins!

DAY 319
Finish What You Begin

We say they are happy because they did not give up. You have heard about Job's patience, and you know the Lord's purpose for him in the end. You know the Lord is full of mercy and is kind.

James 5:11 NCV

Jesus finished what He began, and so should you. Jesus didn't give in, and neither should you. Jesus did what was right, and so should you.

Are you facing something that is hard for you to do? If so, you may be tempted to quit. If so, remember this: whatever your problem, God can handle it. Your job is to keep working until He does.

DAY 320
Be Hopeful

We have this hope—like a sure and firm anchor of the soul—that enters the inner sanctuary behind the curtain.

Hebrews 6:19 HCSB

Are you a hope-filled girl? Hopefully so!

When you stop to think about it, you have lots of reasons to be hopeful: God loves you, your family loves you, and you've got a very bright future ahead of you. So trust God, and be hopeful. When you do, you'll be a happier person . . . and God will smile.

See the Good in Others

See to it that no one repays evil for evil to anyone, but always pursue what is good for one another and for all.

1 Thessalonians 5:15 HCSB

Do you ever make mistakes? Of course you do! Even if you're a very good person, you're bound to make a mistake or two—everybody does.

When you do something you shouldn't have done, here are some things you can do:

1. Apologize to the people you've hurt, and ask for their forgiveness; 2. Fix the things you've messed up or broken; 3. Don't make the same mistake again; 4. Ask God for His forgiveness (which, by the way, He will give to you instantly); 5. Get busy doing something you can be proud of. 6. Don't be too hard on yourself . . . even if you made a mistake, you're still a very, very special person!

DAY 322
Love Everybody

But love ye your enemies, and do good, and lend, hoping for nothing again; and your reward shall be great, and ye shall be the children of the Highest....

Luke 6:35 KJV

It's easy to love people who have been nice to you, but it's very hard to love people who have treated you badly. Still, Jesus instructs us to treat both our friends and our enemies with kindness and respect.

Are you having problems being nice to someone? Is there someone you know whom you don't like very much? Remember that Jesus not only forgave His enemies, He also loved them . . . and so should you.

DAY 323
Telling the Truth

Jesus answered, "I am the way and the truth and the life. No one comes to the Father except through me."

John 14:6 NIV

Sometimes, telling the truth is hard, but even then, it's easier to tell the truth than it is to live with the consequences of telling a lie. You see, telling a lie can be easier in the beginning, but it's always harder in the end! In the end, when people find out that you've been untruthful, they may feel hurt and you will feel embarrassed.

So make this promise to yourself, and keep it: don't let lies rob you of your happiness. Instead, tell the truth from the start. You'll be doing yourself a big favor, and you'll be obeying the Word of God.

DAY 324
Time with God

Careful planning puts you ahead in the long run; hurry and scurry puts you further behind.

Proverbs 21:5 MSG

How much time do you spend getting to know God? A lot? A little? Almost none? Hopefully, you answered, "a lot."

God loved this world so much that He sent His Son to save it. And now only one real question remains for you: what will you do in response to God's love? God deserves your prayers, your obedience, and your love—and He deserves these things all day every day, not just on Sunday mornings.

The Power of Positive Friendships

Light shines on those who do right; joy belongs to those who are honest. Rejoice in the Lord, you who do right. Praise his holy name.

Psalm 97:11-12 NCV

If you'd like to build a positive life, find positive friends. If you'd like to live a godly life, seek the fellowship of godly friends. If you'd like to live passionately, prayerfully, and purposefully, spend time with people who are already living passionate, prayerful, purposeful lives. Soon, you'll discover that you will inevitably become more and more like the people who surround you day in and day out.

In choosing your friends, you set your course for the future. So choose carefully . . . very carefully.

God Solves Problems

Since God assured us, "I'll never let you down, never walk off and leave you," we can boldly quote, God is there, ready to help; I'm fearless no matter what. Who or what can get to me?

Hebrews 13:5-6 MSG

Do you have a problem that you haven't been able to solve? Welcome to the club! Life is full of problems that don't have easy solutions. But if you have a problem that you can't solve, there is something you can do: turn that problem over to God. He can handle it.

God has a way of solving our problems if we let Him; our job is to let Him. God can handle things that we can't. And the sooner we turn our concerns over to Him, the sooner He will go to work solving those troubles that are simply too big for us to handle.

If you're worried or discouraged, pray about it. And ask your parents and friends to pray about it, too. And then stop worrying because no problem is too big for God; not even yours.

DAY 327
God's Plans

God is working in you to help you want to do and be able to do what pleases him.

Philippians 2:13 NCV

God has plans for you...big plans. To understand those plans, you must study God's Word and seek His will for your life. When you do, you'll be amazed at the marvelous things that God will do.

DAY 328
The Best Day

This is the day the LORD has made. We will rejoice and be glad in it.

Psalm 118:24 NLT

What is the best day to celebrate life? This one! This day and every day should be a time for celebration as we think about all the things God has done for us.

Tomorrow morning, when you wake up, take time to count your blessings. And then, be sure to enjoy yourself. Every day is a gift from your Heavenly Father . . . SO CELEBRATE!

DAY 329
What a Friend

And I am convinced that nothing can ever separate us from his love. Whether we are high above the sky or in the deepest ocean, nothing in all creation will ever be able to separate us from the love of God that is revealed in Christ Jesus our Lord.

Romans 8:38–39 NLT

Jesus loves you very much. And you should love Him, too. When you invite Jesus into your heart, you can be sure that He will prepare a place for you in heaven.

Jesus has promised that heaven will be a wonderful place, a place where you will be protected forever.

Jesus is the best friend this world has ever known. Let Him be your friend, too. His love lasts forever. So, what are you waiting for? Welcome Him into your heart right now.

An Example for Others

We're Christ's representatives. God uses us to persuade men and women to drop their differences and enter into God's work of making things right between them. We're speaking for Christ himself now: Become friends with God; he's already a friend with you.

2 Corinthians 5:20 MSG

What kind of example are you? Are you the kind of girl who shows other people what it means to be kind and forgiving? Hopefully so!!!

How hard is it to say a kind word? Not very! How hard is it to accept someone's apology? Usually not too hard. So today, be a good example for others to follow. Because God needs people, like you, who are willing to stand up and be counted for Him. And that's exactly the kind of example you should try to be.

Making the Most of Our Talents

Do not neglect the spiritual gift that is within you....
I Timothy 4:14 NASB

Face it: you've got a collection of talents that need to be improved. All people have special gifts—given by the Father above—and you are no exception.

Today, make a promise to yourself that you will earnestly seek to discover the talents that God has given you. Then, practice your talents and make them grow. Finally, be sure to share your gifts with the world. After all, the best way to say "Thank You" for God's gifts is to use them.

Blessed to Be a Blessing

God has given gifts to each of you from his great variety of spiritual gifts. Manage them well so that God's generosity can flow through you.
I Peter 4:10 NLT

Jesus said, "It is more blessed to give than to receive." That means that we should be generous with other people—but sometimes we don't feel much like sharing. Instead of sharing the things that we have, we want to keep them all to ourselves. That's when we must remember that God doesn't want selfishness to rule our hearts; He wants us to be generous.

Are you lucky enough to have nice things? If so, God's instructions are clear: you must share your blessings with others. And that's exactly the way it should be. After all, think how generous God has been with you.

DAY 333
Thanks for the Memories

I give thanks to my God for every remembrance of you.

Philippians 1:3 HCSB

In his letter to the Philippians, Paul wrote to his distant friends saying that he thanked God every time He remembered them. We, too, should thank God for the family and friends He has brought into our lives.

Today, let's give thanks to God for all the people who love us, for brothers and sisters, parents and grandparents, aunts and uncles, cousins, and friends. And then, as a way of thanking God, let's obey Him by being especially kind to our loved ones. They deserve it, and so does He.

DAY 334
The Roadblock

Those who show mercy to others are happy, because God will show mercy to them.

Matthew 5:7 NCV

If you're unwilling to forgive other people, you're building a roadblock between yourself and God. And the less you're willing to forgive, the bigger your roadblock.

If you really want to forgive someone, pray for that person. And then pray for yourself by asking God to help you forgive. Don't expect forgiveness to be easy or quick, but with God as your helper, you can forgive . . . and you will.

DAY 335
No Regrets

Don't let your spirit rush to be angry, for anger abides in the heart of fools.

Ecclesiastes 7:9 HCSB

When you're angry, you will be tempted to say things and do things that you'll regret later. So don't do them! Instead of doing things in a hurry, slow down long enough to calm yourself down.

Jesus does not intend that you strike out against other people, and He doesn't intend that your heart be troubled by anger. Your heart should instead be filled with love, just like Jesus' heart was . . . and is!

Listen to Your Conscience

I always do my best to have a clear conscience toward God and men.

Acts 24:16 HCSB

Your conscience is a little feeling that will usually tell you what to do and when to do it. Pay attention to that feeling, and trust it.

If you slow down and listen to your conscience, you'll usually stay out of trouble. If you listen to your conscience, it won't be so hard to control your own behavior. Why? Because most of the time, your conscience already knows right from wrong. So don't be in such a hurry to do things. Instead of "jumping right in," listen to your conscience. In the end, you'll be very glad you did.

DAY 337
Who Controls You?

Be imitators of God, therefore, as dearly loved children.

Do you try hard to control yourself? If so, that's good because God wants all His children (including you) to behave themselves.

Sometimes, it's hard to be a well-behaved girl, especially if you have friends who don't behave nicely. But if your friends misbehave, don't imitate them. Instead, listen to your conscience, talk to your parents, and do the right thing . . . NOW!

DAY 338
Telling the Truth

Don't ever forget kindness and truth. Wear them like a necklace. Write them on your heart as if on a tablet.

Proverbs 3:3 NCV

When we're dishonest, we make ourselves unhappy and we let other people down. It's easy to see that lies always cause far more problems than they solve. Lies, no matter what size, are never part of God's plan for our lives, so we must tell the truth about everything.

Have you ever said something that wasn't true? When you did, were you sorry for what you had said? Probably so.

Happiness and honesty always go hand in hand. But it's up to you to make sure that you go hand in hand with them! And besides, when you always tell the truth, you don't have to try and remember what it was that you said!

DAY 339
The Search for Wisdom

If you don't know what you're doing, pray to the Father. He loves to help. You'll get his help, and won't be condescended to when you ask for it. Ask boldly, believingly, without a second thought. People who "worry their prayers" are like wind-whipped waves. Don't think you're going to get anything from the Master that way, adrift at sea, keeping all your options open.

James 1:5-8 MSG

Would you like to have the kind of the wisdom that only God can give? If so, ask Him for it! If you ask God for guidance, He will not withhold it. But here's a word of warning: You will not acquire God's wisdom without obeying His commandments . Why? Because God's wisdom is more than just a collection of thoughts; it is, first and foremost, a way of life.

Wisdom is as wisdom does. So if you sincerely seek God's wisdom, don't be satisfied to learn something; make up your mind to become something. And then, as you allow God to remake you in the image of His Son, you will most surely become wise.

DAY 340
Listen to God

Continue to ask, and God will give to you. Continue to search, and you will find. Continue to knock, and the door will open for you.

Matthew 7:7 ICB

God has many things He wants to tell us. And for starters, He wants us to be loving, kind, and patient, not rude or mean!

The Bible tells us that God is love and that if we wish to know Him, we must have love in our hearts. Sometimes when we're tired, angry, or frustrated, it may be hard for us to be loving. Thankfully, anger and frustration are feelings that come and go, but God's love lasts forever.

If you'd like to become a more patient person, talk to God in prayer, listen to what He says, and share His love with your family and friends. God is always listening, and He's ready to talk to you . . . now!

DAY 341
A Pure Heart

Keep your eyes focused on what is right, and look straight ahead to what is good.

Proverbs 4:25 NCV

Where does a good attitude begin? It starts in our hearts and works its way out from there. Jesus taught us that a pure heart is a wonderful blessing. It's up to each of us to fill our hearts with love for God, love for Jesus, and love for all people. When we do, good things happen.

Sometimes, of course, we don't feel much like feeling good. Sometimes, when we're tired, or frustrated, or angry, we simply don't want to have a good attitude. On those days when we're feeling bad, it's time to calm down . . . and rest up.

Do you want to be the best person you can be? Then you shouldn't grow tired of doing the right things . . . and you shouldn't ever grow tired of thinking the right thoughts.

Golden Rule

Do for other people the same things you want them to do for you.

Matthew 7:12 ICB

Some rules are easier to understand than they are to live by. Jesus told us that we should treat other people in the same way that we would want to be treated: that's the Golden Rule. But sometimes, especially when we're tired or upset, that rule is very hard to follow.

Jesus wants us to treat other people with respect, kindness, courtesy, and love. When we do, we make our families and friends happy . . . and we make our Father in heaven very proud.

Do the Right Thing . . . and the Kind Thing

Let everyone see that you are gentle and kind. The Lord is coming soon.

Philippians 4:5 NCV

Sometimes, it's so much easier to do the wrong thing than it is to do the right thing, especially when we're tired or frustrated. But, doing the wrong thing almost always leads to trouble. And sometimes, it leads to BIG trouble.

When you do the right thing, you don't have to worry about what you did or what you said. But, when you do the wrong thing, you'll be worried that someone will find out. So do the right thing, which, by the way, also happens to be the kind thing. You'll be glad you did, and so will other people!

DAY 344
The Wonder of Heaven

Be glad and rejoice, because your reward is great in heaven.

Matthew 5:12 HCSB

The Bible makes this important promise: when you give your heart to Jesus, you will live forever with Him in heaven. And Jesus told us that His house has "many mansions" (John 14:1-3).

Even though we don't know everything about heaven, we do know this: heaven will be a wonderful place, a place of joy and wonder, a place where we will be reunited with our loved ones and with God. It's wonderful to think about . . . and a priceless gift from God.

Kindness Is a Choice

Love is patient; love is kind.

1 Corinthians 13:4 HCSB

Kindness is a choice. Sometimes, when we feel happy or hopeful, we find it easy to be kind. Other times, when we are sad or tired, we may find it much harder to be kind. But the Bible teaches us to be kind, even when we don't feel like it.

So do everybody (including yourself) a big favor: try to be kind all the time. It's the smart choice and the right thing to do.

What Is Patience?

Therefore, God's chosen ones, holy and loved, put on heartfelt compassion, kindness, humility, gentleness, and patience.

Colossians 3:12 HCSB

The dictionary defines the word "patience" as "the ability to be calm, tolerant, and understanding." Here's what that means: the word "calm" means being in control of your emotions (not letting your emotions control you). The word "tolerant" means being kind and considerate to people who are different from you. And, the word "understanding" means being able to put yourself in another person's shoes.

If you can be calm, tolerant, and understanding, you will be the kind of person whose good deeds are a blessing to your family and friends. And that's exactly the kind of person that God wants you to be.

DAY 347
Learning the Importance of Obedience

You must follow the Lord your God and fear Him. You must keep His commands and listen to His voice; you must worship Him and remain faithful to Him.

Deuteronomy 13:4 HCSB

When you learn to control your actions and your words, you will find it easier to obey your parents, your teachers, and your Father in heaven. Why? Because in order to be an obedient person, you must first learn how to control yourself— otherwise, you won't be able to obey very well, even when you want to.

When you learn the importance of obedience, you'll soon discover that good things happen when you behave yourself. And the sooner you learn to listen and obey, the sooner those good things will start happening.

DAY 348
Helping Others

Never walk away from someone who deserves help; your hand is God's hand for that person.

Proverbs 3:27 MSG

Jesus told the story of the "Good Samaritan," a man who helped a fellow traveler when no one else would. We, too, should be good Samaritans when we find people who need our help.

So always look for people who need a helping hand or a smile . . . and give them both.

DAY 349
Want More Patience?
God Can Help!

Smart people are patient; they will be honored if they ignore insults.

Proverbs 19:11 NCV

Are you a perfectly patient person? If so, feel free to skip the rest of this day's reading. But if you're not, here's something to think about: If you really want to become a more patient person, God is ready and willing to help.

God is always ready to help you become a better person. In fact, the Bible promises that when you sincerely seek God's help, He will give you the things you need. So, if you want to become a more patient person, bow your head and start praying about it. Then, rest assured that with God's help, you can change for the better . . . and you will!

DAY 350
Christ's Peace

Peace I leave with you. My peace I give to you. I do not give to you as the world gives. Your heart must not be troubled or fearful.

John 14:27 HCSB

The beautiful words of John 14:27 remind us that Jesus offers us peace, not as the world gives, but as He alone gives. We can accept His peace or ignore it. When we accept the peace of Jesus Christ into our hearts, our lives are changed forever, and we become more loving, patient Christians.

Christ's peace is offered freely; it has already been paid for; it is ours for the asking. So let us ask . . . and then share.

When Things Go Wrong

I do not consider myself yet to have taken hold of it. But one thing I do: Forgetting what is behind and straining toward what is ahead, I press on toward the goal to win the prize for which God has called me heavenward in Christ Jesus.

Philippians 3:13-14 NIV

When things don't turn out right, it's easy for most of us to give up. But usually, it's wrong. Why are we tempted to give up so quickly? Perhaps it's because we're afraid that we might embarrass ourselves if we tried hard but didn't succeed.

Here's something to remember: if you're having a little trouble getting something done, don't get mad, don't get frustrated, don't get discouraged, and don't give up. Just keep trying . . . and keep believing in yourself.

When you try hard—and keep trying hard—you can do amazing things . . . but if you quit at the first sign of trouble, you'll miss out. So here's a good rule to follow: when you have something that you want to finish, be brave enough (and wise enough) to finish it . . . you'll feel better about yourself when you do.

Are You Feeling Upset or Worried? Pray About It!

I want men everywhere to lift up holy hands in prayer, without anger or disputing.

1 Timothy 2:8 NIV

If you're feeling upset, what should you do? Well, you should talk to your parents and there's something else you can do: you can pray about it.

If there is a person you don't like, you should pray for a forgiving heart. If there is something you're worried about, you should ask God to give you comfort. And as you pray more, you'll discover that God is always near and that He's always ready to hear from you. So don't worry about things; pray about them. God is waiting patiently to hear from you. . . and He's ready to listen NOW!

Trusting the Quiet Voice

In quietness and trust is your strength.

Isaiah 30:15 NASB

Whenever you're about to make an important decision, you should listen carefully to the quiet voice inside. Sometimes, of course, it's tempting to do otherwise. From time to time you'll be tempted to abandon your better judgment by ignoring your conscience. Don't do it!

Instead of ignoring that quiet little voice, pay careful attention to it. If you do, your conscience will lead you in the right direction—in fact, it's trying to lead you right now. So listen . . . and learn.

DAY 354
When We Don't Understand

Immediately the father of the child cried out and said with tears, "Lord, I believe; help my unbelief!"

Mark 9:24 NKJV

Even a good man like Moses couldn't always understand the mysteries of God's plans. And neither can we. Sometimes, people who do nothing wrong get sick; sometimes, innocent people are hurt; sometimes, bad things happen to very good people. And just like Moses, we can't always understand why.

But the good news is this: We will have an eternity to have all our questions answered when we get to heaven. And until then, we've simply got to trust God.

Learning to Be More Obedient

Here is my final advice: Honor God and obey his commands.

Ecclesiastes 12:13 ICB

Learning how to control yourself helps you become a more obedient person. So the more you learn about self-control, the better.

Learning how to control yourself is a good thing. Self-control helps you at home, at school, and at church. That's why parents and teachers are happy to talk about the rewards of good behavior.

If you want to learn more about self-control, ask your parents. They'll help you figure out better ways to behave yourself. And that's good for everybody . . . especially you!

The Right Thing

For the Kingdom of God is not just fancy talk; it is living by God's power.

1 Corinthians 4:20 NLT

Doing the right thing is not always easy, especially when we're tired or frustrated. But, doing the wrong thing almost always leads to trouble. And sometimes, it leads to BIG trouble.

When you do the right thing, you don't have to worry about what you did or what you said. But, if you are dishonest—or if you do something that you know is wrong—you'll be worried that someone will find out. So do the right thing; it may be harder in the beginning, but it's easier in the end.

DAY 357
The Time to Talk to God Is Now

Then if my people who are called by my name will humble themselves and pray and seek my face and turn from their wicked ways, I will hear from heaven and will forgive their sins and heal their land.

2 Chronicles 7:14 NLT

God promises that He hears your prayers—every one of them! So if you want to say something to God, you can start praying (with your eyes open or shut).

Whatever your need, no matter how great or small, pray about it and never lose hope. God is not just near; He is here, and He's ready to talk with you. Now!

DAY 358
The Choice to Rejoice

Shout with joy to the LORD, O earth! Worship the LORD with gladness. Come before him, singing with joy.

Psalm 100:1-2 NLT

Are you one of those kids who has made the choice to rejoice? Hopefully so. After all, if you're a Christian, you have plenty of reasons to be joyful.

So today, think about this: God has given you too many blessings to count, but you can certainly count some of those blessings. Your job is to honor God with your prayers, your words, your behavior, and your joy.

DAY 359
Don't Be Afraid to Ask Questions

When doubts filled my mind, your comfort gave me renewed hope and cheer.

Psalm 94:19 NLT

When you're not sure about something, are you willing to ask your parents what you should do? Hopefully, when you have a question, you're not afraid to ask.

If you've got lots of questions, the Bible promises that God—like your parents—has answers, too.

So don't ever be afraid to ask questions. Both your parents and your Heavenly Father want to hear your questions . . . and they want to answer your questions as soon as you ask.

DAY 360
The Right Time

He has made everything beautiful in its time. He has also set eternity in the hearts of men; yet they cannot fathom what God has done from beginning to end.

Ecclesiastes 3:11 NIV

Sometimes, the hardest thing to do is to wait. This is especially true when we're in a hurry and when we want things to happen now, if not sooner! But God's plan does not always happen in the way that we would like or at the time of our own choosing. Still, God always knows best.

Sometimes, even though we may want something very badly, we must still be patient and wait for the right time to get it. The right time, of course, is determined by God, not by us.

DAY 361
Self-Control Matters

So prepare your minds for service and have self-control. All your hope should be for the gift of grace that will be yours when Jesus Christ is shown to you.

1 Peter 1:13 NCV

Learning how to control yourself is an important part of growing up. The more you learn about self-control, the better. Self-control will help you at home, at school, and at church. That's why parents and teachers are happy to talk about the rewards of good self-control. And that's why you should be excited about learning how important it is to look before you leap . . . not after!

DAY 362
When Homework Should Be Done

We can't afford to waste a minute, must not squander these precious daylight hours in frivolity and indulgence, in sleeping around and dissipation, in bickering and grabbing everything in sight. Get out of bed and get dressed! Don't loiter and linger, waiting until the very last minute. Dress yourselves in Christ, and be up and about!

Romans 13:13-14 MSG

Sooner or later, you'll start getting homework, and when that day comes, you'd better be ready because that's when you'll really need lots of self-control! Usually, homework isn't hard to do, but it takes time. And sometimes, we'd rather be doing other things (like playing outside or watching TV). But, when we put off our homework until the last possible minute, we make it hard on ourselves.

Instead of putting off your homework, do it first. Then, you'll have the rest of your time to have fun—and you won't have to worry about all that homework.

DAY 363
Giving to Your Church

In everything I did, I showed you that by this kind of hard work we must help the weak, remembering the words the Lord Jesus himself said: "It is more blessed to give than to receive."

Acts 20:35 NIV

When the offering plate passes by, are you old enough to drop anything in it? If you are, congratulations! But if you're not quite old enough to give money to the church, don't worry—there are still lots of things you can share!

Even when you don't have money to share, you still have much to give to your church. What are some things you can share? Well, you can share your smile, your happiness, your laughter, your energy, your cooperation, your prayers, your obedience, your example, and your love.

So don't worry about giving to the church: even if you don't have lots of money, there are still plenty of ways you can give. And the best time to start giving is NOW!

DAY 364
Safety Matters

The prudent see danger and take refuge, but the simple keep going and suffer from it.

Proverbs 27:12 NIV

Self-control and safety go hand in hand. Why? Because a big part of self-control is looking around and thinking things through before you do something that you might regret later.

Remember the saying "Look before you leap!"? Well if you want to live safely and happily, you should look very carefully before you decide whether or not to leap. After all, it's easy to leap, but once you're in the middle of your jump, it's too late to leap back!

DAY 365
Celebrating Life

Celebrate God all day, every day. I mean, revel in him!

Philippians 4:4 MSG

Do you feel like celebrating? Hopefully so! Are you expecting God to do wonderful things? Hopefully so! Are you happy about your family, your friends, and your church? Hopefully so! After all, God loves you, and that fact should make you very happy indeed. So treat this day as a big celebration . . . because that's exactly what it should be.

This is the day the LORD has made;
let us rejoice and be glad in it.

—

Psalm 118:24 NIV